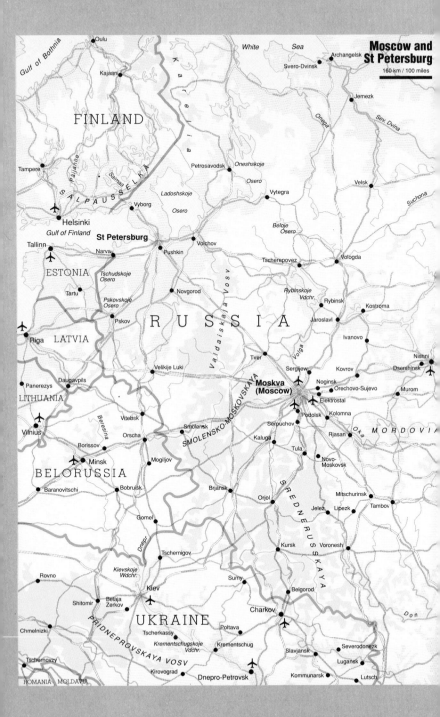

Moscow and St Petersburg

160 km / 100 miles

Gulf of Bothnia

Oulu

Kajaani

White Sea

Archangelsk

Svero-Dvinsk

Jemezk

FINLAND

K a r e l i a

Onega

Sev. Dvina

Tampere

Päijänne

Saimaa

SALPAUSSELKÄ

Petrosavodsk

Oneshskoje Osero

Vytegra

Beloje Osero

Velsk

Suchona

Helsinki

Gulf of Finland

Vyborg

Ladoshskoje Osero

St Petersburg

Volchov

Tscherepovez

Vologda

Tallinn

Narva

Pushkin

Rybinskoje Vdchr.

Rybinsk

Kostroma

ESTONIA

Tschudskoje Osero

Novgorod

V a l d a i s k a j a   V o s v

Jaroslavl

Ivanovo

Tartu

Pskovskoje Osero

Pskov

R U S S I A

Volga

Tver

Nishni

Dsershinsk

Riga

LATVIA

Velikije Luki

Sergijew

Kovrov

Murom

Panerezys

Daugavpils

Beresina

Moskva (Moscow)

Noginsk

Orechovo-Sujevo

LITHUANIA

Vitebsk

Smolensk

SMOLENSKO-MOSKOVSKAYA

Elektrostal

Vilnius

Orscha

Serpuchov

Podolsk

Kolomna

Oka

M O R D O V I A

Borissov

Minsk

Mogiljov

Kaluga

Tula

Rjasan

Novo-Moskovsk

Baranovitschi

Bobruisk

Brjansk

Orjol

S R E D N E R U S S K A Y A

Mitschurinsk

Lipezk

Tambov

BELORUSSIA

Gomel

Dnepr

Jelez

Voronesh

Tschernigov

Kursk

Don

Rovno

Kievskoje Wdchr.

Sumy

Belgorod

Shitomir

Belaja Zerkov

Kiev

Charkov

Chmelnizki

UKRAINE

PRIDNEPROVSKAYA VOSV

Tscherkassy

Poltava

Severodonezk

Tschernovzy

Krementschugskoje Vdchr.

Krementschug

Slavjansk

Lugansk

Kirovograd

Dnepro-Petrovsk

Kommunarsk

Lutsch

ROMANIA MOLDAVIA

MOSCOW

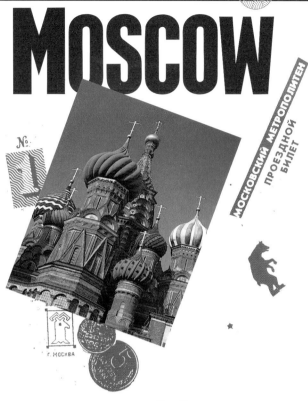

Written and Presented by **Elena Romanova**

Elena Romanova

INSIGHT
pocket
GUIDES

Insight Pocket Guide:
MOSCOW

Directed by
Hans Höfer

Managing Editor
Andrew Eames

Editorial Consultant
Ann Lavelle

Photography by
Jimmy Holmes

Design Concept by
V. Barl

Design by
Carlotta Junger

© **1993 APA Publications (HK) Ltd**

All Rights Reserved

Printed in Singapore by
Höfer Press (Pte) Ltd
Fax: 65-8616438

Distributed in the United States by
Houghton Mifflin Company
2 Park Street
Boston, Massachusetts 02108
ISBN: 0-395-68227-4

Distributed in Canada by
Thomas Allen & Son
390 Steelcase Road East
Markham, Ontario L3R 1G2
ISBN: 0-395-68227-4

Distributed in the UK & Ireland by
GeoCenter International UK Ltd
The Viables Center, Harrow Way
Basingstoke, Hampshire RG22 4BJ
ISBN: 9-62421-574-X

Worldwide distribution enquiries:
Höfer Communications Pte Ltd
38 Joo Koon Road
Singapore 2262
ISBN: 9-62421-574-X

DOBRO POSHALOVAT!

 Welcome! When I was a child growing up in Moscow I used to see the Intourist buses driving around loaded with 'enemies of the people' all clutching guide books that glorified the achievements of the Soviet Union. We were warned against these 'dangerous subversives', but if the truth were told, the tourists' faces peering through the glass looked anything but threatening.

The notion of a foreigner wandering at will through Moscow (for whom this book is designed) is still shocking to some of the older generation – and you may well find yourself being watched surreptitiously as you travel on the Metro or the buses.

In the few years since glasnost and perestroika, we have had to come to terms with a lot of unpalatable facts. Even our pride in the beauty of our city has taken a knock; we mourn the loss of so many pre-revolutionary landmarks.

My aim in creating the itineraries in this book is to show you something of everything: the major sights of the old Russia – the Kremlin, St Basil's, Red Square – as well as those of new Russia – the White House, McDonald's, the flea-markets. And a few Soviet monuments in-between. Wherever you go, I pick out appropriate eating and drinking venues. And please be patient – we are still not fully accustomed to coping with tourism.

Now that I am a radio and magazine journalist and have travelled in Europe, I can understand that Moscow may seem closed to outsiders. But anyone with a little imagination can see what it once was, and what it can become again.

Moscow is tough, even if you have credit cards and currency. Western friends – particularly Anne Lavelle, who helped me put this book together – tell me visitors either love or hate this city. My itineraries are frank – this isn't a typical tourist guide. I can assure you, however, that you will be welcome, and an open mind is the first thing you should remember to bring with you. If you do that, you're in for an unforgettable experience – believe me.

Welcome – Dobro Poshalovat! – Elena Romanova

Contents

Preceding pages:
Moscow overview

Maps

Following pages:
Here's looking at you, kid

Building a Kremlin

Why a cluster of wooden huts on the banks of the Moskva River was chosen as the site of a fortress, or *kremlin,* in 1156, wasn't recorded, but it probably had something to do with the location – on an elevation above a river that wound its way through a series of minor hills, then doubled back on itself, creating a natural fortification. At the time, Duke Yuri Dolgorukiy was looking for an outpost to hinder the Tartar Golden Horde's attacks on the Suzdal-Vladimir principality, whose capital at the time was in Ukrainian Kiev.

The 12th century Kremlin

Two years after 'founding' Moscow, the Duke seized the throne of Kiev and spent the rest of his life ruling the principality. But in the short time he was around, he not only raised a fortress (albeit a wooden one), but also encouraged the trade that would help the fledgling city make its mark on the world.

The *kremlin* was little more than a stockade where a periodic market was held, and the Golden Horde burned it at frequent intervals (torching Moscow was practically a Tartar sport right up until the late 16th century, when the Poles adopted the pastime). There doesn't seem to have been any kind of ruler around for almost 130 years (or maybe they were too insignificant to merit a mention in records), but just before the Tartars' second bonfire, Daniel Nevsky turned up and claimed the title of Prince of Muscovy. To help reinforce the original *kremlin*, he ordered the construction of a series of fortified monasteries around Moscow. The result was a kind of wheel-shaped grouping of fortified religious houses with the *kremlin* as hub. Over the centuries, the spaces in between the 'spokes', or roads, were filled in by housing.

Daniel's efforts paid off to some extent, and the city wasn't burned for 110 years. In the meantime, Daniel's son Ivan (nicknamed *kalita* – moneybags – on account of his careful financial management) was awarded the title of Grand Prince by the Tartars following his conscientious efforts in gathering taxes for them. While collecting tribute, he also managed to buy or conquer neighbouring lands, so that Moscow became the main city of a growing principality.

Tartars torched Moscow in 1238

Ivan Kalita was ambitious and he realised the importance of the Orthodox church in his grand scheme. The then Metropolitan (bishop) was like-minded and managed to organise the relocation of the Holy See from Kiev to Moscow. The city's prestige was greatly enhanced by the move and the Russian rulers' close alignment with Orthodoxy began.

The next big name in early Muscovite history is Prince Dmitry. When he ascended the throne as an eight-year-old child in 1359, the Tartars grew restive. Dmitry appealed for help to the holy man, Sergius of Radonezh, who had built a small monastery in a forest clearing some

70km (44 miles) from Moscow. Sergius was so well respected that he managed to rally all the local princelings to Dmitry's banner and the Tartars were soundly beaten at the Battle of Kulikovo in 1380. Dmitry thus consolidated his position as premier prince in the region, and Moscow began to take on the aspect of a real city.

It was during Dmitry's reign that the *kremlin* acquired its first stone wall and began to warrant a capital letter. The city flourished as more and more merchants moved in, and was well on its way to becoming a major trading centre. It was still subject to taxation by the Tartars, but this came to an end during Ivan III's rule. Ivan ascended the throne in 1462 and was the first prince of Muscovy to assume the title of *tsar*, the Russianised word for 'caesar'.

Known as 'the Great', Ivan interpreted the fall of Constantinople to the Tartars as a sign from God that Moscow was destined to be the third Rome. Ivan felt his new imperial status needed a fitting backdrop. He called in Italian architects to build a new Kremlin to replace Dmitry's rather humble palace. Three cathedrals replaced the old wooden structures and the present Kremlin took the place of the wooden stockade. The three churches continued to symbolise tsarist power until 1917, and each played a specific role in the pomp and ceremony that surrounded the monarchy – tsars were crowned in the Uspensky, matched in the Blagoveshchensky, and dispatched in the Arkhangelsky.

Because of Ivan's belief that he was the true and only inheritor of imperial and Christian Rome, the ties between Church and State were pulled even tighter. The Patriarch lived in the Kremlin along with the tsar and other noble families, and acted as advisor to the crown. This relationship lasted until Peter the Great curbed the power and influence of the Church, and it reached its zenith when Mikhail Romanov was elected tsar. His father had become a priest and was later appointed Patriarch – a relationship between Church and State that bore more resemblance to the Rome of the de Medici than to St Peter's city.

Moscow in the 18th century

The Birth of Red Square

Although frequently plagued by the Black Death, cholera and the Tartars, Moscow prospered. The nobility began building palaces and trade produced a wealthy merchant class. More and more European traders arrived in the capital, bringing not only new goods, but also new ideas to the Russian court. The commercial Kitai Gorod district to the east of the Kremlin sprang up and the space in-between was paved as a marketplace. Its size and proportions earned it the name of *krasnya*, which translates literally as red but also means beautiful or best. Red Square thus became the city's central marketplace and in its heyday had some 400 wooden stalls. For centuries, merchants peddled their wares on the site. But the whole place was a permanent fire hazard – the great Trinity Fire that destroyed much of the old city in 1737 actually started here.

Ivan the Terrible

The city centre began to assume its present form following the crowning of Ivan the Formidable (otherwise known as 'the Terrible', especially in Hollywood). He earned the nickname (*grozny* in Russian) through prowess in the battlefield. In his early years, he wasn't particularly terrible, but he suffered from the kind of paranoia that is common in autocrats and dictators (Stalin had it, too). When his beloved wife died suddenly, he suspected poison, and that's when he changed for the worse. Yet Ivan did a lot to enrich and embellish Moscow. He built St Basil's and endowed numerous other churches. His grandfather and namesake had already forced the nobility out of their Kremlin palaces and into Kitai Gorod and the area to the north, which became known as the White City after the colour of its walls (the present Boulevard Ring marks their original site).

The most popular street in the White City was Tverskaya and the nobility vied for plots along this ancient trade road. (Sadly, most of the palaces and churches they built were destroyed in the 1930s to make way for Stalin's remodelling plans.) The tsars soon saw the importance of this street and utilised it periodically for their own ceremonial purposes. Even after Peter the Great transferred the capital to St Petersburg, and relegated Moscow to provincial-town status, the road was still used for imperial entries into the city.

After Ivan's death, his son Fedor was crowned tsar. The poor man was an imbecile and most of the affairs of state were left to his brother-in-law, Boris Godunov of the Mussorgsky opera fame. Although not an aristocrat, Boris proved a sound ruler and on Fedor's death in 1598 he was elected tsar. But he wasn't liked, and the great noble families felt slighted that a mere 'gentleman' was running the country. To spread ill-feeling they dug up an old rumour that Boris had murdered Fedor's infant son Dmitry (the baby had died in mysterious circumstances in 1591). Consequently when three years into the reign famine struck, Boris was blamed, and when a rather ill-favoured young man turned up with a Polish army at his back, claiming to be Fedor's dead son, the nobles believed him. As the Polish army, now swelled with Russians and Cossacks, advanced on Moscow, Boris dropped down dead. 'Dmitry' was installed as tsar.

Dmitry the Fake

It soon became clear that not only was the Polish contingent settling in for the duration, but also that 'Dmitry' was a Catholic. Within months, Dmitry the Fake was murdered and the country fell into chaos. Many nobles proclaimed themselves tsar, but no one managed to secure the title.

While the Russians were squabbling among themselves, two men rode to Sergiev Posad in an attempt to rally patriots to their banner. It was a historic move as the monastery was synonymous with Russian unity and national endeavour. The Poles heard about it and besieged the walled monastery for 16 months before decamping back to the safety of the Kremlin. The two men were a surprising alliance – one was a prince, the other a butcher; Prince Pozharsky and Minin (there's a statue to them outside St Basil's). They drove out the Poles, and Mikhail Romanov, the son of a nobleman, was elected tsar. His dynasty was to rule for 304 years.

Decline and Fall

The Romanovs produced every conceivable kind of ruler – capable, inspired, innovative, insane, cruel – but all had one thing in common: they were absolute autocrats. The courts of the Romanov tsars were hotbeds of intrigue and political manoeuvring, but during their rule Moscow flowered into one of the greatest and most cultured cities in the world.

Increasing mercantile contacts with foreign parts led to an influx of artistic influences from abroad. Russian nobles soon began to take their own Grand Tours and many began remarkable collections of European and Russian art. Peter the Great encouraged a

Chagall's 'I and the Village'

westward-looking attitude, and when he built his new capital, St Petersburg, on swamp land taken from the Swedes at the turn of the 18th century the design and planning were European. Peter's move to his namesake city meant the nobility and most of the major commercial enterprises followed him.

As St Petersburg grew in magnificence, Moscow declined into a provincial town where nothing much happened. This state of affairs continued until Peter repealed the compulsory service laws. Freed from their enforced stay in St Petersburg, the nobles and merchants gradually began to return to Moscow. They brought with them all kinds of new ideas on architecture and the arts. Many brought the art collections they had accumulated on their Grand Tours.

A Second Flowering

The 19th century was a time of national revival in the arts. Old crafts and art forms, such as ceramics and iconography, came back into vogue. The revitalisation of Russian art went hand in hand with the development of a new tradition combining both Russian and European influences which in the early 20th century produced artists such as Malevitch, Kandinsky and Chagall. They were inspired by late 19th-century writers like Turgenev and Chekhov and composers Mussorgsky and Tchaikovsky. Opera and ballet at the Bolshoi were daring expressions of a new and exciting movement in the world of dance and music; Diaghilev's Ballet Russe went on to take European capitals by storm.

But even as Moscow relived its former glory, and regained some of its old glamour, disaffection began to take hold. While revolutionaries placed bombs, the arts expressed a general dissatisfaction with society through the works of futurist poets, such as Vladimir Mayakovsky, Anna Akhmatova and Maxim Gorky.

Post-Revolutionary Moscow

For a decade after 1917, it seemed as though the Revolution which had swept away the very fabric of Russian society had done something similar in the arts. By 1932 most of the avant-garde movements that had influenced the arts both at home and abroad – architecture, painting, poetry, literature – were dead, as were many of their practitioners, often by their own hand. Others fled into exile. Meanwhile, in Moscow Stalin's wedding-cake architecture and

On the Arbat

horrendous high-rises ran amok.

Social-realism descended on the capital (Lenin had reinstated Moscow as premier city), mocking art and artists. It lasted until a new disaffection took hold in the late 1960s, 1970s and early 1980s. For decades, the work of Soviet writers, painters and musicians was dismissed outside the USSR and satellite states as pandering to a bureaucratic ideology rather than exploring artistic expression. Artists who tried to break through the bureaucracy were censored and even imprisoned. Yet beneath the surface of an art world that was unimaginative but 'ideologically sound', the underground movement of 'subversive' writers and artists, such as Brodsky and Solzhenitsyn, gained in momentum. Change was inevitable.

In the Wake of Glasnost

Since the collapse of the Soviet Union in the wake of the Gorbachev and Yeltsin reforms, everyday life in Moscow has been transformed. Whereas only a few years ago, people queued and jostled to buy anything they could find in the dusty, mainly empty shops, now the streets are packed with eager, brightly-dressed vendors. Some of these proffer just a pair of old shoes or a bottle of vodka, but the more sophisticated traders brandish bottles of Western perfume, Benetton sweaters and CDs. Capitalism has been thoroughly embraced. The queue outside McDonald's is now longer than the one to Lenin's tomb.

But economic freedoms have caused gross inequalities. Citizens working in new capitalist ventures are prospering while pensioners and state employees have been reduced to paupers. Galloping inflation means that in between selling a house and buying a new one, the value of the roubles made can plummet so far that buying any sort of property is suddenly out of the question.

But most Muscovites and Russians prefer to square up to the terrible problems of perestroika rather than return to the Communist system, as the demise of the coup by the old guard in August 1991, when troops and tanks clanked into Moscow, made clear. Muscovites have survived Tartar hordes, Polish occupation, Napoleon and even Stalin. They believe that by making one last tremendous effort their city can at last take its rightful place among the great metropolises of the world.

Historical Highlights

1147 Chronicles mention a settlement on the city's site.

1156 Duke Yuri Dolgurukiy 'founds' the city of Moscow.

1238 The city is razed by fire at the instigation of the Tartar Baty-khan.

1272 Daniel Nevsky is the first to assume the title of Prince of Moscow.

1323 The city becomes the seat of the Orthodox Church in Russia (transferred from Vladimir).

1326 First stone cathedral is built.

1382 The Tartars are back again – this time under Tokhtomush-khan. The city is destroyed.

1475–78 Italian architect Fiorovanti builds the Assumption Cathedral in the Kremlin.

1485–95 Italian builders construct the present Kremlin walls.

1534–38 Kitaigorod (the merchant quarter adjoining Red Square) is walled.

1547 Ivan the Terrible becomes Tsar of Russia.

1554–60 St Basil's is erected.

1563 Moscow's first printed book appears.

1571 The city is sacked again by Tartars – this time from the Crimea.

1586–93 The 'White City' of Moscow is walled along the site of the present Boulevard Ring.

1589 Orthodox Patriarchate is set up in Moscow.

1598 Boris Godunov is elected tsar by the Zemsky Sobor (the Russian equivalent of medieval parliament).

1601–03 Famine strikes the city. Ivan the Great commissions the Kremlin Bell Tower.

1610–12 Moscow is invaded by the Poles.

1613 Mikhail Romanov is elected Tsar of Russia and begins the dynasty that will rule until 1917.

1703 *News About Military and Other Matters* becomes the city's first newspaper.

1713 Peter the Great moves the Russian capital to St Petersburg.

1737 The 'Trinity Fire' destroys the Kremlin.

1755 Russia's first university is founded in Moscow.

1812 Napoleon invades the city and finds it burning (fired by the departing population). On departure, in October, he tries unsuccessfully to blow up the Kremlin.

1824 Opening of the Bolshoi (literally 'big') Theatre.

1851 The first railway line, the Nikolaevskaya, is built.

1866 Moscow Conservatory opened.

1870 The State Duma (parliament) meets for the first time in Moscow.

1896 Nicholas II and Alexander Fyodorovna are crowned tsar and tsarina in the Kremlin; the Khodynka calamity occurs during the ceremony (the population had gathered for free food and drinks at the Khodynka Field and hundreds were suffocated and crushed in the rush).

1905 The December uprising.

1906 The first general election for seats in the State Duma are held.

1912 The Alexander III Museum of Fine Arts (now the Pushkin) opens.

1914 Russia enters World War I against Germany.

1917 Russia signs a separate peace. Following the October Revolution the Bolsheviks take power. Lenin moves the capital back to Moscow; start of the Civil War.

1922 The Union of Soviet Socialist Republics is officially declared.

1924 Lenin dies and his mausoleum is erected on Red Square.

1920s and 1930s Massive new building projects (including the metro system) lead to the destruction of vast areas of old Moscow.

1935 First metro line inaugurated.

1941 The USSR enters World War II against the Axis.

1954 Khrushchev becomes General Secretary (equivalent of president) and introduces the first glasnost.

1962–82 Krushchev is toppled and replaced by Brezhnev; the era of stagnation.

1985 Gorbachev pushes through glasnost ('openness') and perestroika (new economic policies). Moscow looks for its heritage and churches are reopened.

1991 August coup – Boris Yeltsin leads popular resistance resulting in the end of communism and the establishment of the Russian Federation.

1992 Moscow reverts back to old street names and continues the search for its history.

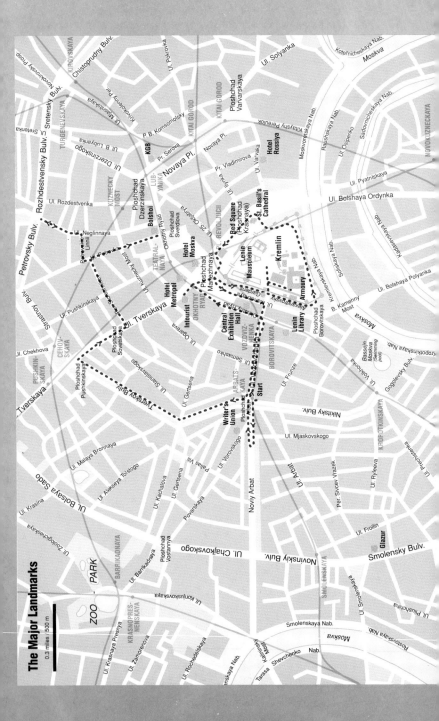

The Major Landmarks

0.3 miles / 500 m

ZOO - PARK

Day itineraries

DAY 1

The Major Landmarks

Breakfast at the Biryusa Cafe and Kulinariya. Tour of the Kremlin Armoury and St Basil's. A walk round Red Square. Lunch at El Rincon Espanol. Shopping around Tverskaya Ulitsa and Noviy Arbat. Dinner at Glazur or the Writer's Union.

Before you set out try to make your dinner reservation for tonight (see the end of this itinerary for my restaurant recommendations) as you may be disappointed if you just turn up on spec. With this evening's arrangements fixed up, head for Arbatskaya (Арбатская) Metro station and when you exit, you'll see Noviy Arbat (Новый Арбат – it may still be called Kalininsky Prospekt on some maps) across the busy street in front of you. Stop off for a light breakfast at the Biryusa Cafe and Kulinariya at No 29 (rolls and pastries on the ground floor, coffee and tea on the first). This will also introduce you to the unique way of paying for things in Russian stores. You decide what you want (all prices are clearly marked), you go to the cash desk and tell the cashier the price (take a small note pad with you if you don't speak Russian and write it down). You then pay for it and take your receipt which you take to the counter where they give you the goods.

If you need something more substantial than coffee and rolls, you can also try the extensive breakfast buffet at the Metropol Hotel on Okhotny Ryad Ulitsa (Охотный Ряд Улица, formerly Prospekt Marksa) – Metro Okhotny Ryad, where you'll pay around \$20. Both are within easy walking distance of the Kremlin.

A visit to **Red Square/ Kremlin** (Красная Площадь/Кремль) is essential for anyone wanting some

Guard change in Red Square

The Kremlin and Moskva river

insight into Russia and the now defunct Soviet Union. No other part of the city combines the brilliance and opulence of the old Empire with the pomp and iconography of the new. As there is so much to see in the Kremlin, we're going to concentrate on the Armoury and its diamond collection. Because this is Russia, you can't just walk up to the gate and go in. You have to buy a ticket for the Armoury at the **Intourist** office in the Intourist hotel (tickets for other Kremlin buildings are on sale at a kiosk near the Trinity Gate entrance).

Coming from breakfast at the Metropol, if you exit from the Metro at Okhotny Ryad, cross the square and, keeping the Hotel Moskva (big building bang in the middle of the four-lane traffic flow) to your left, walk just around the corner to Intourist on Tverskaya Ulitsa (Тверская ул.). If you're coming from Arbatskaya Station, turn right out of the station, walk down to the lights and turn left at the Lenin Library. Follow the square about 150m (500ft) to the corner and turn left. You can't miss Intourist: it's the high-rise that looks like a badly-maintained 1960s tower block. You can also pick up currency tickets at Intourist for concert and theatre performances, but as these are now available for rubles at most venue box offices it's no longer essential to get them from Intourist.

Go back to the corner. The square in front of you is Manezhnaya Ploshchad (Манежная пл., formerly 50-letya Ok-tyabrya). Cross the square (if you jay-walk, you'll get a ticket, so use the subways). From the corner, you can see the **Alexandrovsky Gardens** (Алехандровский Сад) running around the Kremlin and it is these we

At the tomb of the Unknown Soldier

need to get into. Cut through the gardens, past the eternal flame for the unknown soldier. You'll probably become entangled in a wedding group, as this is a popular backdrop for wedding albums.

The Trinity Gate and the only public entrance to the Kremlin is ahead of you. The **Armoury** is a relative newcomer to the complex. Built in 1851 by Konstantin Ton as an art museum, it stands on the site of a 16th-century armoury – hence the name. You'll find the tsarist crown jewels (imperial crown, mace, sceptre) here, along with other trappings of old Russia. The tsarist symbol is the double-headed eagle; the Armoury is full of them. Until very recently, you would rarely have seen it elsewhere. The golden thrones and dinner services merit special attention, but there's so much that glitters and shines you will probably want to spend at least a couple of hours here. When your eyes are well and truly dazzled, rest them by wandering freely through the grounds and admiring the exteriors of the other museums. These include four former cathedrals, the Patriarch's Palace and the Grand Palace, which was used for state occasions during the days of tsarist rule.

Tsarist riches in the Armoury

Exit through the Trinity Gate and turn left into the gardens towards the Moskva River. Circle the walls to **St Basil's**. Stand in line at the small kiosk for a ruble ticket – the cathedral has a poor collection of frescoes, but you have to go in because it's St Basil's. While you're waiting, check out the circular stone elevation on your left – it was the place of execution in the Middle Ages and was later used for reading tsarist decrees. The monument in front of the main entrance commemorates Minin and Pozharsky, the two men who organised the liberation movement against the Poles in the early 17th century. It was the first sculpture completely paid for by public subscription.

St Basil's is actually nine churches, and its real name is the Pokrovsky Cathedral. Built by Ivan the Terrible to commemorate a series of victories against the Tartars in the 1550s, it was nicknamed St Basil's after a holy man who predicted Ivan would murder his first-born and suffer eternal damnation. Basil the Blessed's

St Basil's

warning came as the Russians prayed for victory against the Tartars on Red Square, and when the old man died he was buried in the Trinity Cathedral that stood originally on the Pokrovsky site. Although only one church is dedicated to him, the whole building has always been popularly known as St Basil's.

If you have a strong stomach and relish trying local food, when you leave St Basil's pick up a hot, meat-filled dumpling and a can of something soft from one of the numerous vendors that crowd every corner. Cross Red Square (in Russian the word meaning 'red' was also used for beautiful or the best; the political connotation was a 'happy' coincidence), keeping St Basil's behind you. The Lenin Mausoleum is on your left. Hotel Rossiya is down the street from the cathedral to your right down Varvaka Ulitsa (Варварка ул., formerly Racina Ul.) and has currency restaurants and cafés if you can't face the rather greasy looking pasties. Alternatively, you can grab a hamburger and Pepsi at one of the kiosks outside the Intourist Hotel. If it's cold and you want to sit in some comfort, have a currency lunch at the **El Rincon Espanol** in the Hotel Moskva on Manezhnaya Ploshchad (Манежная пл.). It's the giant twin-towered building on the east side of the square. The hotel was built to accommodate People's Deputies from the Republics in the Stalin era and if you manage to get a full frontal view, you'll see the towers don't match. The story goes that Stalin had to approve every building plan and in this case he initialled two. The architects were too frightened to ask which he preferred, so they built half and half.

If you didn't manage to get through to this evening's choice of restaurants this morning, you can try calling again now.

Entertaining the crowds in Red Square

Who said there was nothing in the shops? The whole area around the Kremlin is full of familiar Western stores – Benetton, Christian Dior, Yves Roches. Lancome – some for rubles, some for currency. If you've been doing any people-watching, you won't be surprised by the glut of cosmetics stores. You'll find most Russian-made goods are pretty poor quality and many of the souvenirs are downright tacky. But there are exceptions.

After browsing a bit, make for Noviy Arbat by walking down Manezhnaya, keeping the Kremlin on your left. Ahead you'll see the **Central Exhibition Hall** or Manege; you can't miss it, it's the huge, rather shabby looking mustard-coloured building with a classical facade. Pass it and Noviy Arbat is the second turning on your right. Walk up the street, past the House of Friendship on the right (it's the odd white turreted building fronting the street at No 16). Cross Nikitsky Bulvar (Никитский бульв., formerly Suvorovsky), and check out **Dom Knigi** at No 26 Noviy Arbat for wonderful children's and antiquarian books, icons and prints. Music buffs will love Melodiya on the same street (No 14) – look for classical CDs

Bronze relief of Gogol's statue

here. There's a very good antique shop just off Noviy Arbat on Vakhtangova Ulitsa (Вахтангова ул., on the left if you're walking up from the Kremlin), but if you buy any antiques, make sure you're given the right paperwork for export or you may find your wonderful samovar confiscated at customs.

Afterwards make your way back to Nikitsky by walking 50m (160ft) to the end of Vakhtangova and turning left onto the Arbat. Walk to the top of this pedestrian street market and cross Noviy Arbat onto Nikitsky (there's a post office on the corner). Pop into the tiny park dominated by a brooding statue of Gogol to see his characters worked in subtle bronze relief at the base. If you read Russian, the building on your right is a great public library. Cross Nikitsky Bulvar into the park that divides it into a dual carriageway and rest on a bench, watching the chess players that congregate here on fine days.

Now for more shopping. Follow Nikitsky Bulvar up to Gertsena Ulitsa (Герцена ул.), where the TASS building is on your right, and cross into the continuation of the park – this is Tverskoy Bulvar (Тверской бульв.). Follow it up to Pushkinskaya Ploshchad (Пушкинская пл.). Turn right onto Tverskaya and walk around 500m (1,600ft) until you come to Stoleshnikov Pereulok (Столешников пер.), third on your left. Walk up this street until you reach Petrovka Ulitsa (Петровка ул.). Cross the street, turn left and then take the first street on your right which will bring you to Neglinnaya Ulitsa (Неглинная ул.) and **Noty** (at No 14). Climb to the second floor and browse through a treasure trove of sheet music – from balalaika to Beatles and Beethoven – and opera scores. These make very special and original souvenirs. Check out prices here before giving in to the temptations of street vendors; you'll probably find the stores are cheaper. Small co-operative shops are opening every day – their wares are pretty similar,

Souvenirs on the street

but you may find an ex-Red Army watch at bargain prices, or hand-embroidered linen and furs. Sadly the Russian preoccupation with what are considered Western goodies – Donald Duck chewing gum, Turtles stickers, etc. can make these small enterprises a disappointment. Had enough? If you've been looking at your map occasionally, you'll see we've actually come almost a full circle – the Metropol is at the south end of Petrovka, and the Bolshoi is just opposite. Now that you are almost a native, you've earned a rest before your first Moscow dining experience.

Because prices have gone through the roof lately, it isn't as difficult as it used to be to get a table at a restaurant, especially if you're paying the bill with hard currency. As already said, you should have booked your table this morning and almost all the restaurants only accept reservations for the same day. If you speak no Russian whatsoever, you may find yourself eating at joint-venture currency restaurants throughout your stay. I could give you a whole list of useful phrases, but these are pretty useless if you can't understand what the other person is saying in reply. For full details of how to book, and a vocabulary to help read the menu, see the *Eating Out* section later in this book.

Try **Glazur**, a rather up-market currency co-op at Smolensky Bulvar 12 (Смоленский бульв.), about 70m (230ft) down from the Stalin wedding-cake Ministry of Foreign Affairs building, where they serve Russian *zakuski* (starters) as they are supposed to be (Tel: 248 4438). **The Writer's Union** (Tel: 291 2169 or 291 1515) used to be an elite preserve, but its crisp linen, crystal and silver can now be handled by anyone with enough currency to afford the Gothic splendour and delicate cuisine (Povarskaya Ulitsa 52 – Поварская ул., formerly Vorovskogo), Metro Arbatskaya, then cross Nikitsky onto Noviy Arbat and it's the second street on the right).

Old Russia

Breakfast at the Georgian House. Tour of the bishop's palace Krutitzkoye Podvorye. Picnic lunch. An afternoon in a monastery. Decadence at the Banya steam baths. Dinner at U Nikitskikh Vorot or Strastnoi 7.

Once again, try to make your dinner reservation before leaving (see the end of this itinerary for details). For this tour you should pack your toilet bag, towel and a pair of plastic sandals or flip-flops (you will find out why later). Take the purple-line Metro to Proletarskaya (Пролетарская); your best bet is to get into the last metro car because it will set you down close to the right exit. When you come through the barrier turn left into the subway and use the far right-hand stairs. The orange brick building that looks fairly new and well-kept is the **Georgian House** and its café will serve you coffee, tea, the now ubiquitous Slim-Fast drinks, and a bun or pastry (closed in winter). You can also buy bread in the store on your left. The main shop entrance is on the corner to your right – pick up cheese here for a picnic at Spasso-Andronikovsky this afternoon.

The Novospasskiy Monastery

Once you've fortified the body, it's time for the soul. Walk down the street and to your right you'll see the gleaming onion towers of the **Novospasskiy Monastery**. There was a time when you could go inside, but the complement of monks has shrunk to five and there are no facilities for visitors. But you can wander around the walls of this 15th-century 'new'

Saviour's cathedral. You may have noticed that there is a Saviour's Gate in the Kremlin but no church of that name. The reason is that in the mid-1400s, Prince Ivan III decided to move the monastery from the rather crowded Kremlin to this location. At the time, all convents and religious houses served a dual purpose – as places of worship and as fortifications, so this site's elevation above the Moskva River was considered ideal. But once the monks had moved

in, Ivan promptly forgot about them, and the place fell into disrepair until Mikhail Romanov became tsar in 1613. He and his son Alexei finished the building. It's an incongruous complex amidst the grim high-rise blocks, yet it still manages to dominate the whole area.

The same cannot be said for the **Krutitzkiy Podvorye**. You'd never find it if you didn't know it was there. Walk down from the monastery back to Krestyanskaya Ploshchad (Крестьянская пл.), with the river on your right. Cross the road and follow the small park on Bolshoi Kamenskaya Ulitsa up to the end (about 75m/250ft). The decrepit looking lot ahead is where you turn right – into Krutitzkye Val Ulitsa (Крутицкий Вал ул.). Plan on spending no more than an hour here.

The curator at the former Krutitzkiy Metropolitan's (bishop's) residence will tell you that renovation is complete. You could be forgiven for thinking it has only just started. The overgrown gardens, continual sound of hammering and shabby-looking buildings belie the fact that an architect – Peter Baranovskiy – spent 35 years piecing this place back together from semi-ruins. You must see this, because it is a monument to the Russian love/hate relationship with the Orthodox Church – and

Tiled facade on Krutitzkiy Podvorye

not only in the present century. The earliest mention of the complex is 12th-century. Like all monasteries all over the world, it also served as a hostelry for travellers and was once outside Moscow's city walls (it's 6½km/4 miles from the Kremlin). As you come in through the gates, the building on your left, with its proud staircase, is actually two churches – the Assumption, and St Peter's and Paul's. Walk around the far side and look at the green tiled ceramic facade that incorporates bunches of ripe grapes and vine leaves (symbolising Christ). It was made in six months during the 17th century and incorporates more than 1,000 tiles. Take one of the two vaulted archways to bring you into what was once a formal garden fronting the Metropolitan's palace. To your right is a small **museum** with pewter religious ornaments, many of which were hidden for decades during the Soviet regime (because they are marked with the tsarist double-headed eagle, they were proscribed objects) and only recently reappeared.

The Podvorye complex's history is chequered. It remained the Metropolitan's headquarters for centuries (after the Patriarch, the Metropolitan is still the most important in the Russian Orthodox Church's hierarchy). But the tsarist love affair with the Church soured under Catherine the Great, and the complex was confiscated. It fell into ruins and was then burnt by Napoleon's troops in 1812. Subsequently rebuilt, it was turned into flats for badly-heeled peasants, and people lived here until the 1970s. After World War II, architect Baranovskiy began his slow and painstaking renovation. The staff are trying desperately to continue the work, but there is a chance it will be returned to the Church at some point in the future.

If you're interested, you can attend a

Keeping out the cold

service in one of the churches – times are posted at various points. When you leave the museum on your right, you'll see a high barbed-wire fence, the perimeter of a military prison. Its presence contributed to the survival of the Metropolitan residence as no new building plans were approved for this site on security grounds. The monastery itself also functioned as a place of detention – the 19th-century revolutionary Gertsen was held here by the tsarist regime. Give the museum shop a miss – it has the usual range of plastic icons, crude bread boards and the kind of gonks popular with teenagers in the 1960s and the staff are ill-informed (one blew chewing-gum bubbles while providing me with inaccurate information on the history).

Retrace your steps back to the Metro and either eat your picnic in the small park – it's popular with dog owners – or keep it until you get to Spasso-Andronikovsky. To get there, take the Metro one stop to Taganskaya (Таганская). Follow the change boards to the yellow line whose station here is called Marksistskaya (Марксистская), again get into the last car, and go one stop to **Ilicha Ploshchad** (Илича пл.). Exit, turn right, then right again. You'll find yourself on a small square – follow the right turn down Tulinskaya Ulitsa (Тулинская ул.) until you see a park on the right-hand side of a square. Cross the park and enter the **Spasso-Andronikovsky** monastery through the gates at the back end of the park. Follow the street along until it bears left and you will see the gates ahead of you. To do the monastery justice, allow a couple of hours at

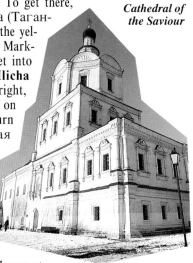

Cathedral of the Saviour

least. If the frescoes at St Basil's disappointed you, this is the place to see the real thing. The **Russian Icon Museum** located in three of the former monastery buildings is named after Andrei Rublev, arguably the best and certainly the most famous Russian iconographer. He was a monk here and his works once adorned the interior of the **Cathedral of the Saviour** (1420–27) to your left when you enter the gates, but only a fragment in the arched window over the altar now remains. Rublev is buried in the small church directly ahead of you when you enter the gates.

If you can't manage three whole buildings of icons, make sure you see the **Seminary**, the first building on your right as you come through the gates. It houses the oldest and most costly collection in Russia, many of the exhibits dating back to the 15th century. Pride of place is taken by a 13th-century icon of the Saviour, which makes it even earlier than the cathedral. It was discovered in the 1960s under a couple of 18th and 19th-century overlays. Then,

skirting the cathedral to your left, cross the courtyard to the **church of Archangel Michael,** a rare example of grand baroque where every level is decorated in an individual style – it is simply sumptuous. This is also the restoration studio which is sometimes open to the public. Visit on a Saturday afternoon and you will be able to hear the Siren choir perform medieval chants in the monastery.

Are your feet killing you? Still got your toilet bag? We're going to finish off with a leisurely steam bath at the gloriously decadent **Sandunovskaya Banya** (Сандуновская Баня). You already know how to change lines at Marksistskaya for Taganskaya. It's two stops from here to Kuznetsky Most (Кузнецкий Мост). Leave the station and turn up Rozhdestvenka Ulitsa (Рождественка ул.), then take the first on your left (Neglinniy 1st Pereulok – Неглинный 1-й пер.) and you'll see a sign: Banya (Банна).

If you've been feeling dizzy from all the fabulous frescoes, these ornate 19th-century baths, built by a wealthy merchant especially for his courtesans, will ease you gently back into form. A manicure and massage are also available if you want them. Unlike neighbouring Finns and Swedes, the Russians are not into mixed bathing. I can't tell you what the men's baths are like, but the women's have an amazing cold water pool complete with marble statues and ornately carved wooden framed mirrors. As you go in, you'll be given a large bath sheet, but you'll have to take your own thongs or plastic sandals. These are compulsory, not only because of hygiene, but also because the sauna floor is hot enough to take the skin off the soles of your feet.

Feeling hungry? **Strastnoi 7** (Tel: 299 0498) is a short walk away. Turn right out of the Banya entrance, then right onto Neglinnaya Ulitsa (Неглинная ул.). Take the first on your left

Lenin's Mausoleum has a night-time changing of the guard

into Petrovskiye Linii Ulitsa (Петровские Линии ул.). At the end of the street, turn right onto Petrovka Ulitsa (Петровка ул.) and follow the road up, passing Moskvina Ulitsa on your left. The next turning is Strastnoi Bulvar (Страстной бульв.) and, you guessed it, the restaurant is at No 7. It's a classy currency place, popular with business people, and the traditional Russian food served here is consistently good – try the blinies and caviar (if you can afford them).

The other choice **U Nikitskikh Vorot** is further away, on the corner of Nikitsky and Gertsena Ulitsa (Герцена ул., Tel: 290 4883). The menu has no frills, but the food is solid and the bistro style relaxed – rubles.

If you feel like hitting a night-spot, walk down Gertsena to Manezhnaya (Манежная). Try to time your arrival about 10 minutes before the hour and cross over to Red Square and the **Lenin Mausoleum** for the beautifully choreographed changing of the guard – they still do it. If you go at night, it is less crowded and the spotlights on the Kremlin Wall and St Basil's make it a truly 'Soviet' experience (takes place all year – if you can bear the winter cold).

DAY 3

The Art Trail

Breakfast at the Intourist coffee shop. View Russia's art history heritage at the Tretyakov. A Soviet tragedy. Lunch at the Moscow Yard. Back to the future at the Tropinin. Galleries galore. Dinner at Lazania.

Again, before setting out, remember to make your dinner reservation (see the end of this itinerary for my recommendations). After breakfast at the Intourist coffee shop, take the Metro to Tretyakovskaya (Третьяковская). When you exit, turn left, cross the road and turn left at the corner onto Ordynskiy Tupik (Ордынский Тупик). The **Tretyakov Gallery** is on the corner of the first street on your right. A visit here is strongly recommended, as it traces the history of Russian art from the 11th century onwards. Unfortunately, due to restoration work on the build-

The Tretyakov

Inside the Tretyakov Gallery

ing only a part of this 50,000 piece collection is on show, so limit your time here to a maximum of two hours. The collection begins with Kievan icons and follows the development of this particular art form through to Rublev (his *Trinity* is one of the highlights that shouldn't be missed). During the 17th, 18th and 19th centuries, Russian artists were influenced by European movements, and vice versa. This came to an abrupt end in the 1920s and the museum is the perfect place to see how Russian art became Soviet, inspired by social-realism rather than imagination. Malevitch and Kandinsky are here, but after them sound ideology replaced creative genius as the criterion for a place in museums.

What you get to see will depend on luck more than anything else. The original Tretyakov palace has been closed for renovation for years, and the exhibition space is housed in the Finnish-built 'new' gallery (not to be confused with the New Tretyakov, which is a purely commercial venue). This hosts a lot of special exhibitions but it has been the subject of criticism. Not long ago, there was a scandal involving mis-use of the works in the collection and protests at the State's inability to preserve Russia's artistic heritage. Boris Yeltsin promised action – but we're still waiting.

Retrace your steps back to the Metro corner and turn right onto **Ordynka Bolshaya Ulitsa** (Ордынка Большая ул.) for a very different Moscow experience. Forget the ungainly tower blocks and ostentatious tiered monstrosities of the Soviet era and travel back in time to the elegant 19th century. This is embassy country, so don't be surprised to see African kids riding bicycles along the well-kept pavements – if you're used to a multi-ethnic society, this area will come as a relief from all those consistently pale Slavic faces.

Walk down the right-hand side of the street for around 150m

34

(500ft) and you'll see a white stone wall with a high central entrance. The gates are backed by sheets of metal so you can't see what's behind them. But if you look to your right, you will see a tiny wooden gate (the letters K1 are scratched above in red paint). If it is closed, push it open and follow the railings on your left to the end of the path and you'll see what's hidden from the street.

To Elizaveta's Church

This classical white **church** (Marko-Mariinskaya Obitel) was built by Grand Duchess Elizaveta Fjodorovna, sister-in-law of the last tsar and married to his uncle, Grand Duke Sergei, who was also mayor of Moscow. He was killed by a revolutionary bomb in 1904. It had been a political and not very happy marriage, and after his death Elizaveta turned to religion. Her particular kind of piety took the form of good works. She established this church and a small convent where women could spend retreats and help her at a hospital she founded for the poor.

Her charity and good works made her the equivalent of Mother Theresa during her lifetime, and she was revered as a living saint by the Muscovites. When the Bolsheviks took over, she was arrested along with all the other members of the Tsar's family who hadn't fled the country. She was taken to Alapaevsk in the Urals, imprisoned in a school building and finally thrown down a mine shaft along with a number of her relatives. It took them days to die from their injuries. Only a handful of party *apparatchiks* knew what had happened to her – most people thought she had simply been shot. The true story only emerged a couple of years ago, creating a major scandal as numerous old people recalled her good works. Her church and convent are now being restored.

Continue down the street for lunch at the **Moscow Yard** – in summer you can sit outside under the trees; in the winter the café moves into the steamy basement. The food is simple, uninspired but solid. This is a good spot for mafia-spotting. Watch out for groups of guys in identical designer suits who flash wads of all kinds of cash and drink Western liquor like there was no tomorrow. The café has a good selection of imported beers, Armenian brandies, soft drinks, and also cigarettes. The co-operative store on the first floor sells

Detail, Elizaveta's Church

an unfamiliar brand of Japanese film and rents out Soviet-made cars if you're interested.

Just across from the Moscow Yard at No 39, you'll see another church which is now home to **Art Moderne Gallery**. It's a commercial art show and the standard isn't exceptionally high but if you're doing this in winter, you may want to get in out of the cold. You'll probably be asked to pay for admittance.

Continue down Ordynka to the next corner (Kazachiy 1st Pereulok/ Казачий 1-й пер.) and turn right. Just opposite you'll see a door in the side of the flat building. Pop in

Fresco from St Cather

to see how Muscovites manage to find elusive items, such as shower heads, taps and paint brushes; the tiny room-cum-shop is typical of retail reality in the city. Then cut down to your left past the well-guarded car park – the tenants here are Westerners, so their wheels merit security.

After the crumbling, badly maintained buildings you've seen everywhere else, you may be startled by the chic green-icing and white chantilly town house on your right. In summer, flowering creepers climb gently towards the red tiled roof of this perfectly kept **Tropinin Museum**. I like to tell myself this is how all Moscow will look one day – clean, well-preserved, as if people are making an effort and really care. Now for a bit of museum etiquette. When you enter most museums, the first thing you'll see is a small bench and a box of felt slippers – these are to protect wooden floors from wet snow and high heels. Put these on over your shoes before taking your coat to the cloakroom assistant (you won't be allowed to go round wearing an overcoat).

The Tropinin is actually the city's portrait gallery, covering the 18th and 19th centuries and, though small, you could spend an hour here easily. The works and miniatures on show change from time to time, but Catherine the

Portrait in the Tropinin

Great is a permanent profile in the first room to your left at the top of the stairs – pop into the adjoining room for a quick look at the rather bizarre collection of porcelain in the left corner cabinet.

The two rooms on the right of the entrance are devoted almost exclusively to Vasily Tropinin's own works. My personal favourites are in the third room (the occasional table and two chairs in the corner by the door to this room are traditional birch from Karelia and date from the 18th century). The small water-colour portraits aren't of famous people, although there is a Tolstoy daughter here. I love them for their subtle colours and simplicity. The fourth room has two superb books of drawings and water-colours of old Moscow; these will be the nearest you'll get to a hands-on approach in any museum. When you pick up your coat downstairs, ask if they still have packs of postcards depicting paintings from the collection – they should be still three rubles a box which is incredible in these

inflationary days. If you need a toilet, this is probably the cleanest you'll find in the city; there was even soap on the washbasin last time I was here – a rarity in Moscow.

When you leave the Tropinin, turn to your right at the door and walk down to the end of the street. Just before the corner you'll see high rail-

Lazania offers Italian cuisine

ings backed by an overgrown garden and tall unpruned trees. Follow the fence round to the entrance on Ordynka. The church is St Catherine's and it was built between 1763–67 by Karl Blank. It has now been returned to the Orthodox church and restored; check out the fabulous ceiling frescoes (I hope they'll have finished renovating them for your visit). Just down the street to your right on the left-hand side there's a currency café/bar where you can sit down for a while and have a drink before getting ready for dinner.

Lazania (Pyatnitskaya Ulitsa 40/Пятницкая ул.; Tel: 231 1085; hard currency, cash only) is one of the oldest co-operative restaurants. As the name suggests, they make a brave attempt – not always successful – at producing Italian-style food. This is still a very popular eatery with the smart set and foreigners who enjoy the shady terrace where you can dine *al fresco* in the summer months. The easiest way to get there from Ordynka is to walk up to Dobryninskaya Ploshchad (Добрынинская пл.) and take the first on your left. This is the right street for Lazania, but the restaurant itself is still a bit of a walk.

Morning Itineraries

1. The Russian Parliament and Soviet Architecture

Checking out the KGB before a late breakfast at Café-Grill No 12. Seeing the sights of the second revolution. A Constructivist dream. Lunch at Vareniki.

Take the Metro to Lubyanka (Лубянка, formerly Dzerzhinskaya) and exit onto the square of the same name. The enormous building

Vacant plinth and KGB headquarters

opposite is KGB **headquarters**. The plinth where secret-police chief Dzerzhinsky's statue once stood is still there; the marble effigy has gone, as has the old name. It has now reverted back to Lubyanka, although this also has some pretty frightening connotations. If you're standing at the Metro exit, you turn left onto Teatralny Proyezd (Театральный пр.) and Okhotny Ryad. Follow the street until you see the Bolshoi on your right, keep going with the Moskva Hotel on your left, cross Tverskaya (formerly Gorky Ulitsa) and head down to the next corner. It's Gertsena Ulitsa (Герцена ул.) and you should turn right here. Follow the road about 150m, passing the Zoological Museum on your right, for a late, very

Soviet breakfast at **Cafe-Grill No 12** (same street number). It is uninspired, and perhaps not ultra hygienic, but Muscovites have been managing for years on the processed cheese sandwiches, sticky buns, strong *chai* (tea) and weak coffee sold here.

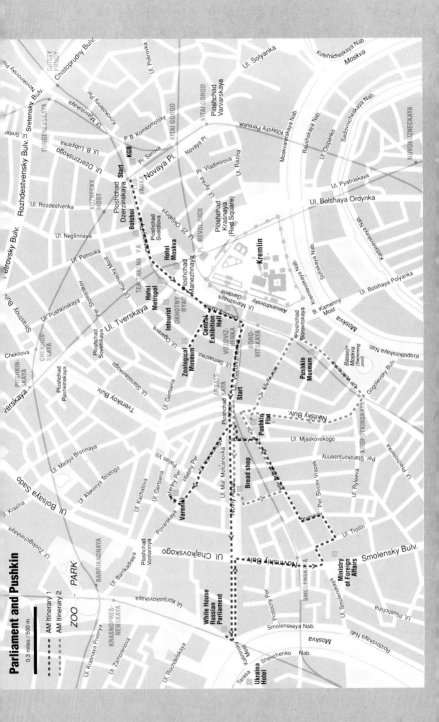

Parliament and Pushkin

0.3 miles / 500 m

- AM Itinerary 1
- AM Itinerary 2

Parliament

Walk back down Gert-sena, cross over to the Ma-nege (alias the Central Exhibition Hall) and pick up trolley bus 2. It will take you down Noviy Arbat to the river. If you get in at the front you'll be able to see the Ukraina Hotel (another Stalin wedding cake on the opposite bank). Get off on this side of the water. Turn right onto the embankment and the 'White House' immediately to your right is the Russian **parliament building** where Boris did it all in 1991.

Perhaps the bombardment of world news since those August days, when Gorbachev suddenly disappeared in true old-fashioned Soviet style, and an unsavoury group of grim-faced politicians and generals took over 'for the sake of the Union', has wiped the memory of the 'second revolution' from your mind. Let's just recap. A coup was organised to oust Gorbachev (which it did, but not the way the plotters had in mind) by a group of conservatives who wanted to return to the old status quo, in which they had all the power, privileges and prerogatives, and the rest of the Soviet people had bread lines. The coup failed because the Muscovites, led by Boris Yeltsin, resisted *en masse* and, after some bloodshed, the army divisions meant to support the plotters and impose martial law mutinied and joined the people on the barricades. Few places outside Moscow actually saw any action; the whole plan was geared to subduing the capital. After its failure, the coup leaders tried to sneak out of the city, but their stretch limousine cavalcade was a little too conspicuous; their ignoble retreat was followed by a vanguard of press and police officers. The plotters were arrested and some are still in prison awaiting trial. A few have already been released on health grounds.

Back to the first revolution. The White House, and the Ukraina across the river, are classic examples of the style of architecture typical of megalomaniacal Soviet power. Yet, in the 1920s, there was a very different movement that flourished in the new Soviet Union, and which would exert a major influence on 20th-century building styles in the West. This so-called Constructivism was to architecture what Kandinsky's graphics were to design, or Malevich's canvases were to painting. The leading exponent of Constructivism was Konstantin Melnikov who dominated Soviet architecture for about 10 years, before falling foul of the regime.

Little remains of this movement, yet if you walk back up Noviy Arbat to Novinskiy Bulvar (Новинский бульв., formerly Chaykovskogo), turn right and head for the Ministry of Foreign Affairs building (a landmark in Stalin's wedding-cake style), a short stroll will take you to one of the most startling buildings in

The Ministry of Foreign Affairs

the city. Walk up the Arbat and take the third street (it's more like an alley) on your right, passing the graffiti homage to rock star Victor Tzoiy. Follow the road around for about 100m (330ft) and you'll find a small cylindrical white house wedged between two crumbling apartment buildings. It is currently being restored and there are plans to turn it into a museum. This is the house Melnikov built for himself and his son still lives there. It is a fine example of what history might have intended for Homo Sovieticus if the early dreams had become reality.

At the end of the street, turn left onto Plotnikov Pereulok, which takes you back to the Arbat. Head up towards the Arbatskaya (Арбатская) Metro station and turn left at Arbatskiy Pereulok (Арбатский пер.). Cross Noviy Arbat, and turn left at Povarskaya (Поварская, formerly Vorovskogo). Walk up Paliashvili Ulitsa (Палиашвили ул.) to Skatertnyy Pereulok (second on the right) for lunch at **Vareniki** (rubles) – no reservations and no frills, but good solid Ukrainian-style dumplings and chicken Kiev. Service is fast, and turnover faster.

2. Pictures of Pushkin

Breakfast at Breadshop No 102. Shopping on the Arbat. A tour of the Pushkin Museum. Pushkin revisited. Lunch on the Arbat.

Get the Metro to Arbatskaya (Арбатская) and head over to Noviy Arbat and **Breadshop No 102** at No 46 for wonderful freshly baked rolls. Pick up a hot drink at one of the numerous kiosks. Slip down any of the side streets on the left of the main road to the Arbat – the pedestrian shopping street where in the early days of glasnost young artists who weren't considered ideologically sound and had no access to the official art circuits tried to sell their work to visitors and Muscovites alike. It evolved into the place for young people to hang out, wear their Levis and leather

jackets, or punk outfits, and rebel against authority in a usually good-humoured way. At the time of the real upheavals following far-reaching perestroika, it was a centre for public debate that outdid London's Hyde Park Corner.

Art on the Arbat

The Pushkin Museum

Sadly, today it is a tourist trap (but with a wealth of small eateries, so start looking for one you like the look of, as we'll be coming back here for lunch). Browse, but don't buy here – save your rubles and currency for the flea market at Izmaylovsky (*see Pick & Mix Option 5*).

If you're feeling lazy, walk down the Arbat to the Metro station and hop the subway to Kropotkinskaya (Кропоткинская). This will mean changing at Borovitskaya (Боровицкая), so walking to the **Pushkin Fine Arts Museum** (Tuesday–Sunday 10am–7pm, closed Monday) will probably be quicker. To do this, turn right at the Arbatskaya end of the Arbat and cross Gogolevskiy Bulvar (Гоголевский бульв.) to pick up Frunze Ulitsa (Фпунзе ул., it's the first street on the left). Follow Frunze to the end at Borovitskaya Ploshchad (Боровицкая пл.) and turn right down the street about half-way up the square (there's only one turning, so you can't miss it). This brings you onto Volkhonka Ulitsa (Волхонка ул.) and the museum is at No 12.

I can't tell you what to see here – that's up to personal taste. But the museum houses an amazing range of periods and styles, ranging from Ancient Egyptian and Byzantine to Picasso, Monet, Rodin, and the best collection of impressionists and post-impressionists in

The Outdoor Swimming Pool

the country. Opened in 1912, the museum was originally designed as a centre where plaster casts of Western sculpture enabled students to study foreign art without leaving the country. After the revolution, Lenin 'nationalised' all private art collections and many are now to be found here at the Pushkin.

When you leave the museum, turn to your right and walk to the end of the street. On your left is the **Moscow Outdoor Swimming Pool** (you're not advised to swim here). This was the original site of Saviour's Cathedral, built to celebrate the Russian victory over Napoleon. The cathedral took 46 years (1837–83) to complete, and only six days to demolish – the marble salvaged from the interior was used to ornament a number of Metro stations. It was one of the first victims of Stalin's plans to remodel Moscow and a new Palace of the Soviets was to be built in its place. Construction began in 1933 but architects and builders soon found out why building the cathedral had taken so long. Every time they dug out foundations, the holes filled with swampy water and 20th-century technology

Pushkin

proved unable to pull off what 19th-century builders had achieved. The gaping hole was finally turned into a swimming pool in the Khrushchev era – a short-sighted move since the vapours it emits are destroying the neighbouring Pushkin collection.

At the end of the street, you'll see the grassy centrepiece that slices the four-lane Gogolevsky Bulvar in two. If you cross over to it, and follow the park to its end, you'll see the Arbatskaya Metro station on your right. Go back onto the Arbat for lunch, stopping first at No 32. This is Pushkin's old **flat**, the only surviving place where he lived. The collection of prints and engravings, paintings and books (including his own works) gives extra interest to the classical Empire-style interior designed in the early 19th century.

3. On the River

Breakfast at the Metropol. A river boat ride. Window shopping on Noviy Arbat. A stop at the Scryabin museum. Lunch at the Novo Arbatsky.

Make for the **Metropol Hotel** on Teatralny Proyezd (Театральный пр. – Metro Okhotny Ryad/Охотный Ряд or Teatralnaya/Театральная) for a hefty buffet breakfast to line your stomach in readiness for the river-boat trip. When you leave the hotel, cross Teatralnaya Ploshchad, keeping the Moskva Hotel to your right, and turn left into Red Square. Continue down the square, taking the road to the left of St Basil's. The horrifying high-rise on your left (whose construction meant pulling down around 30 small churches and other old buildings) is the notorious **Rossiya Hotel**. With over 5,000 beds, it's like a small city in its own right, and has a full complement of currency shops and a Baskin Robbins ice-cream parlour for anyone who hasn't realised that, although the Russian variety usually comes in vanilla flavour only, it can compete with any *gelati* in the world. Keep the Rossiya on

On the Moskva

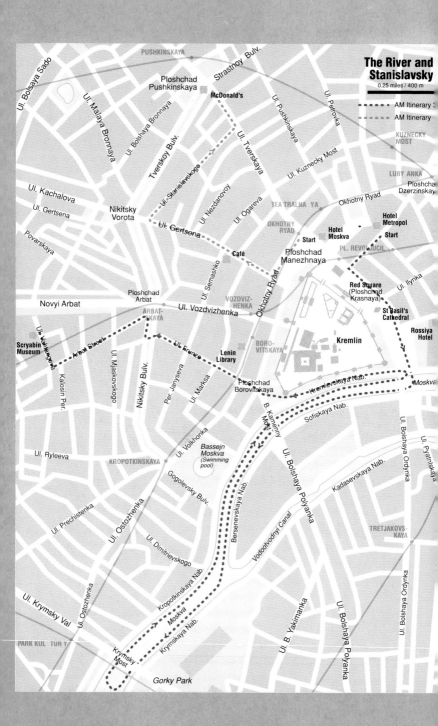

The River and Stanislavsky

0.25 miles / 400 m

····· AM Itinerary 3
····· AM Itinerary

PUSHKINSKAYA

Ul. Bolsaya Sado

Ul. Malaya Bronnaya

Ul. Bolshaya Bronnaya

Ploshchad Pushkinskaya

Strastnoy Bulv.

McDonald's

Ul. Pushkinskaya

Ul. Petrovka

KUZNECKY MOST

Tverskoy Bulv.

Ul. Stanislavskogo

Ul. Tverskaya

Ul. Nezdanovoy

Ul. Ogareva

Ul. Kuznecky Most

LUBY ANKA

Ploshcha Dzerzinskay

Ul. Kachalova

Ul. Gertsena

Nikitsky Vorota

Ul. Gertsena

TEATRALNA YA

Okhotny Ryad

Hotel Metropol

Povarskaya

Ul. Semashko

Café

OKHOTNY RYAD

Start

Hotel Moskva

Start

Ploshchad Manezhnaya

PL. REVOLUCII

Ul. Ilynka

Novyi Arbat

Ploshchad Arbat

Ul. Vozdvizhenka

VOZDVIZ-HENKA

Okhotny Ryad

Red Square (Ploshchad Krasnaya)

St Basil's Cathedral

ARBAT-SKAYA

BORO-VITSKAYA

Rossiya Hotel

Scryabin Museum

Ul. Vahangova

Arbat Street

Ul. Frunze

Lenin Library

Kremlin

Kalosin Per.

Nikitsky Bulv.

Ul. Mjaskovskogo

Per. Janyseva

Ul. Marksa

Ploshchad Borovitskaya

Kremlevskaya Nab.

Moskva

Ul. Ryleeva

KROPOTKINSKAYA

Ul. Volkhonka

Bassejn Moskva (Swimming pool)

B. Kamenny Most

Sofiskaya Nab.

Ul. Bolshaya Ordynka

Ul. Pyatnisks

Ul. Prechistenka

Ul. Ostozhenka

Gogolevsky Bulv.

Ul. Dimitrievskogo

Bersenevskaya Nab.

Kropotkinskaya Nab.

Ul. Bolshaya Polyanka

Vodootvodnyi Canal

Kadasevskaya Nab.

TRETJAKOVS-KAYA

Ul. Krymsky Val

Ul. Ostozhenka

Moskva

Krymskaya Nab.

Krymsky Most

Ul. B. Yakimanka

Ul. Bolshaya Polyanka

Ul. Bolshaya Ordynka

PARK KUL TUR Y

Gorky Park

your left and you'll see the river ahead of you.

Although there is now a currency boat trip leaving once a day at noon from the Ukraina Hotel complete with pseudo-Italian snacks and drinks for wads of hard cash, we're going to be doing what Muscovites do. The boats leave from next to the bridge here every 15 minutes (spring to the end of summer) and stop off at various locations to drop or pick up people. If the day is fine and you want to see the city from a totally different perspective go to the end and return the same way. It looks less crumbling and impoverished from the water, as even the Soviet-era buildings make their own contributions to the sky-line. If you feel like stretching your legs, get off at **Gorky Park** and take a walk, before embarking again to return to the Rossiya landing stage.

When you get off, walk to your left and follow the Kremlin walls along the river to the next bridge. Turn up to the right – the Kremlin gate on your right is used by VIPs, so watch out for stretch limos and ZILs (Russian cars) exiting here. You'll know if someone is about to leave as the GAI (traffic police) bring the whole traffic flow, including pedestrians, to a halt.

Turn onto Borovitskaya Ploshchad (Боровицкая пл.) and, keeping the **Lenin Library** on your right, walk up Frunze Ulitsa to Arbatskaya. The Lenin Library is a typical example of the style of architecture that ousted Constructivism in the late 1920s, when the ideology changed from simplicity to 'giving the proletariat marble pil-

In the Scryabin Museum

lars and classical facades'. From Arbatskaya, turn onto the Arbat and take the fourth on your right at the Vakthangov Theatre into the street of the same name (Вахтангова ул.). The **Scryabin Museum** at No 11 (Wednesday, Friday and weekends noon–6pm, Thursday 10am–4pm, closed Monday and Tuesday) was the composer's home. It remains intact and holds regular Sunday concerts of his music (a programme is posted at the entrance).

Ready for lunch? Go down the steps to get to Noviy Arbat, where you have a choice: the **Irish House** bar on your right or, if you turn to the left and walk to the end of this long grey building, the **Arbat restaurant** on the corner.

Late breakfast at the Oladji café. Browsing the books outside TASS. A tour of the Stanislavksy museum. Checking out original souvenirs. Lunch at McDonald's – no kidding.

Make for Metro Okhotny Ryad (Охотный Ряд). Use the exit for Nasional Hotel and walk along Manezhnaya Ploshchad (Манежная пл.) to the next corner and turn right up Gertsena

Street-stall books

Ulitsa (Герцена ул.). The **Oladji café** is right next door to the Tchaikovsky Conservatory on the left (you can't miss it, there's an immense bronze statue of the composer in a rather unfortunate artistic pose). The café doesn't open until 10am, so try and time your arrival for that time – the tea and coffee will be fresh-made. Afterwards, continue up Gertsena – the rather tatty looking building on the right was a palace in pre-Revolutionary days and it was used by its owner, Zinaida Shakhovkskaya, for artistic soirées. A group of artists are currently trying to revive the magic, so check out the programme at the door. If you like the saccharine sweetness of Russian candy, pop into Confisserie No 18 just across the street and see what they've got.

Gertsena now crosses Nikitsky Vorota Ploshchad (Никитские Ворота пл.) and the TASS building is on the right-hand corner. Budding entrepreneurs have set up book stalls outside; these often have English and other foreign language detective stories and novels along with children's picture books and coffee-table productions on the city.

Turn right here onto Stanislavskogo Ulitsa (Станиславского ул.) and follow the street along to his **museum** at No 6 – this one is a must for theatre buffs. The fact that the street is named after Stanislavsky, the stage-struck merchant who threw up a promising career in textiles to become the founder of the Moscow Art Academic Theatre MKNAT in 1888, recalls the pre-Revolutionary tradition of naming roads and bulvars in the 'cultural' area around the Arbat after prominent artistic figures.

The story goes that Stanislavsky hated the artificiality of the often ham acting prevalent at the time. He worked out plans to set up a new approach to theatre with a friend, Nemirovich-Danchenko, during a marathon 18-hour lunch. His ideas developed into the internationally influential Method school of acting.

The museum is housed in the building Stanislavsky used to set up his Opera Dramatic Group. As you go in, you'll see a programme

of regular Wednesday recitals. If you want tickets, buy them inside the museum.

Leave your coat downstairs and don't forget to put on felt slippers. The main exhibition rooms are up the staircase. Pop into the concert room, with its miniature acropolis stage set and raise your eyes heavenwards for the first of many perfectly-restored painted ceilings in the museum. You should also have a quick look at the Red Room next door which contains book-cases fronted by imitation stained-glass doors depicting knights and courtly scenes – Stanislavsky's other passion. The next room shouldn't be missed. This was his study and is preserved intact (although all the furniture is covered by dust-sheets so you can't actually admire it). It is divided by a rather ponderous book-case and the area behind was used as a 'back-stage' when Stanislavsky was rehearsing new plays or improvisations with his drama troupe.

The ceilings were restored in the 1970s and they are stunning. You can't go into Stanislavsky's bedroom or that of his wife, so peep through the door. The family dining room is at the end of the corridor and contains portraits of his grandparents; if you want to see it, go and stand in front of the door and one of the ladies may come and open it for you. The smell of mothballs is overpowering and, except for the family groups, there's little of real interest here but if you're on a pilgrimage you have to see it.

The cellar contains Stanislavsky's personal collection of artefacts used to help actors get into the right mood. You will also find amazing beaded headdresses from the Volga and some pretty gaudy period costumes that must have looked subtle and refined on stage.

If you still have some stamina before lunch, pop into the small **Museum of Applied Arts** across the street. This is a prime example of art combined with commerce – the big hall on the left is rented to an entrepreneur while the right is still the preserve of *matryoshka* dolls and hand-carved, hand-painted wooden spoons.

When you leave here, turn right and walk to the end of the street. Turn left onto Tverskaya (Тверская) and continue up to Tverskoy Bulvar (Тберской бульвар) – join the line at McDonald's for lunch. Now that inflation has exploded, the queue shouldn't be too long.

One of them is real

Art in the shade, Izmaylovsky Park

5. Shopping in the Park

Breakfast at Izmaylovsky Park. Trip to the biggest and best flea market in town. Open-air lunch in the park (weekends only).

Take the Metro to **Izmaylovsky Park** (Измайловский Парк) station. When you exit, walk around to the back of the building for breakfast at the café – straight Soviet fare here, but it will set you up for bargain hunting. The market was initially begun by the Moscow Soviet authorities as an open-air art gallery. It only became popular when people selling all kinds of bits and pieces moved in. For many years, it was illegal, and the site, usually deep in the park, changed from week to week. But it seems anything goes now, and stalls trip you up as soon as you leave the Metro. You can buy almost anything here – from ex-Soviet uniforms to computer software and, of course, traditional crafted products, such as hand-crocheted woollen shawls and embroidered tablecloths. Prices are high, but not as outrageous as on the Arbat or the corner of Tverskaya.

The park itself was once the grounds of the royal Izmaylovo hunting lodge built by the Romanovs in the early 17th century. Most of the lodge has since disappeared, but the Bridge Tower, a typical example of 17th-century Russian timber and stone architecture, with receding tiers and belts of patterned stone, remains and is worth seeing. The Triple Gates are also extant. This is the royal seat where Peter the Great spent most of his childhood. Exiled from Moscow by the relatives of his half-brother, Tsar Theodore, he is believed to have found the rotting wooden boat that would kindle his lifelong interest in ships in one of the estate's sheds. The boat was probably a gift from Elizabeth I of England to Ivan IV. Nicknamed the 'grandfather of the Russian navy', it is still preserved in a small museum on Lake Pereslavl, near Moscow.

Pick up lunch from one of the *shashlik* vendors who roast juicy chunks of meat on open charcoal fires and buy a drink or ice cream from the strolling entrepreneurs.

Afternoon Itineraries

6. Lenin's Heritage

A tour of the Lenin Museum. Shopping at GUM. An evening at the Bolshoi. Supper at the Savoy Bar to catch up on the news.

The **Lenin Museum** is on the corner of one of the access roads to Red Square, so head for Metro Okhotny Ryad (Охотный Ряд). When you exit from the Metro, make for the tomato-ketchup coloured Gothic edifice on the opposite corner to the Hotel Moskva.

Glass portrait in the Lenin Museum

Entrance is still free. Leave your coat downstairs in the empty cloakroom and make your way to the escalators in the marble ground-floor hall. Ride up to the first floor (second in Russian parlance). What you will find are room upon room of documentary memorabilia and enough of Lenin's overcoats to clothe a small army. All the papers and photos here are copies. After glasnost, the museum's staff removed the originals because they were afraid the population might turn nasty and destroy the place. None of the overcoats are particularly significant; he wasn't shot in any of them, although the authenticity of the bullet that was extracted after the assassination attempt is certified by no less than six physicians, and is surrounded by three great globs of blood-red sealing wax – in room 12 if you're interested.

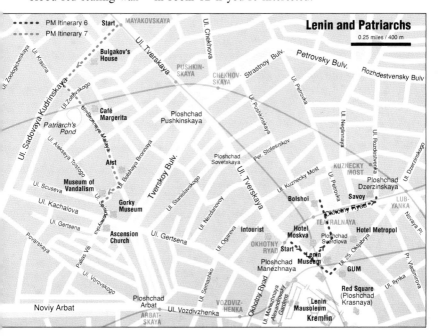

Lenin's Rolls-Royce

As a child, I can remember seeing the giant stained-glass Lenin window on the first floor, where Lenin is depicted in the kind of brash red, yellow and black you normally associate with a badly adjusted, cheap colour television. He looked larger than life then, now he just looks garish. Check out the original Rolls-Royce he used in 1923 – although some claim it too is a copy.

Unless you're a serious student of Soviet iconography, you can give the rest of the rooms on this floor a miss, except for hall 17. For decades, every picture we ever saw of Lenin showed him fresh-faced, wise and healthy looking. Now, as you enter this room, you're taken aback by a sickly-looking Grandfather Ilych partly shrouded by cheese-cloth drapes and seated at the far end – as if he's just walked over from the Mausoleum. All the exhibits, photographs of his final days, are shrouded in the same wispy white fabric giving an eerie feel to the whole room.

Don't miss the ground floor exhibition on Lenin's early life. Skip the first couple of rooms, which describe his idyllic childhood, and move on to the more interesting exhibits, including the fireplace he warmed himself at during his stay at 30 Halford Square in London (presented to the people of the Soviet Union in 1947), a coffee table he used in Copenhagen in 1910, and the reading-room chair he sat on in Geneva's public library. There are a lot of other unique items of this nature; it's well worth studying them, so take your time.

Having spent part of your afternoon with the great man, you may now want to examine the fruits of his ideology. We're off to GUM – the remarkable pastel-painted 19th-century department store with its large and wonderful wrought-iron interior, fountain and hard currency shops.

To get there, leave the Lenin Museum and turn to your left. Go to the corner and turn into the short Istoricheskiy Proyezd (Ис-

Grand interior of the GUM department store

Bolshoi performance

торический пр.) leading to Red Square. GUM (ГУМ) is the building on your right as you turn left at the corner of Nikolskaya Ulitsa (Никольская ул., formerly 25-Letiya Oktyabrya) and Red Square. The small booth on the left-hand corner selling icons against a backdrop of feverish building work marks the spot where Kazan cathedral once stood. A place of pilgrimage, it was destroyed by Stalin in the 1930s. Nothing was built in its place. However, in 1990 an historic procession led by Patriarch Alexis II, Boris Yeltsin and the then-mayor Gavriil Popov left the Kremlin to lay the foundation stone of a new cathedral here.

Retrace your steps to the Lenin Museum, pass it, and you'll see the **Bolshoi** across the square to your right. You can pick up a ruble ticket at the box office. If they have run out of good seats, you could also try the Intourist ticket office in the hotel of the same name on Tverskaya (Тверская).

Performances start at 7pm sharp; don't be late because they won't let you in once the curtain is up. You should be back on the street at around 10pm (during the interval have a glass of *champanskeye* – it's traditional, and maybe a small caviar snack, depending on supplies).

Now for supper. From the front of the Bolshoi, cut through the small garden ahead of you (by the way, this is the gay cruising spot, though be warned, homosexuality is still a capital offence in Russia, and the militia will enforce the law if they see people soliciting openly), and turn left onto Okhotny Ryad, keeping the Metropol on your right. The **Savoy** and its bar are on the

second street on your left (Rozhdestvenka Ulitsa/Рождественка ул.). Before inflation caused endless supplies of food and drink to appear almost overnight at greatly inflated prices, and before we could pick up CNN on our TVs at home, this was the place where Western business types and journalists, and Muscovites with currency, stopped off for a bar meal and a shot of real news. If you're very hungry, place two orders – the portions make nouvelle cuisine look hearty. You can walk in off the street, no reservation needed, and get something to eat and drink while watching CNN on the box.

Try the bar

Pay your respects at Bulgakov's House and a quiet walk around Patriarch's Pond. A quick look at the Museum of Vandalism before a tour of Gorky's art-nouveau reward. Time for divine service. Dinner at Café Margerita.

Bulgakov's masterly satire on relations between people and state, *The Master and Margarita* published in 1969, became a cult book and the rallying cry for a new generation of Russians. Although not exactly suppressed in the Soviet Union, half of the early edition was blanked out by the censors. I never quite understood why that was, as the book is timeless, and the aspects of life he is describing could apply to any time, in any place and not just to the Commun-

Stairwell of Bulgakov's house

ist era. Efforts to set up some kind of monument to the writer were blocked by the Soviet authorities, so people transformed the stairwell of his **house** into an impromptu shrine. To get there head for Metro Mayakovskaya (Маяковская). Turn left out of the exit and walk down the ring road – follow Sadovaya Bolshsaya Ulitsa (Садовая Больжая ул.) onto Sadovaya-Kudrinskaya Ulitsa (Садовая-Кудринская ул.) to number 10/12. Cut through the archway and go into the second entry on your left. Don't be put off by the apparent privacy of the place; the residents are used to people turning up with flowers and even scratching graffiti on the walls.

In his book, Bulgakov incorporated a number of imaginary creatures that make statements the 'real' characters can't. This style of commentary builds on an earlier tradition in Russian literature which uses animals instead of people to observe human behaviour.

When you leave the Bulgakov house, turn left out of the archway and then take the second on your left. This is **Patriarch's Pond** where the writer spent sunny afternoons. The statue dominating this end of the pond is of the 19th-century satirist poet Krylov whose heroes were all animals.

This is my neighbourhood. I grew up just around the corner and this is where I played as a child. Don't be surprised to see people fishing here: the water may look unpromising, but I can remember a booth on the corner that sold carp from the pond when I was small. There used to be black swans too, and you could skate here in the winter. Skirt the pond on the left bank; there's a kiosk that often has foreign newspapers and magazines, cigarettes, soft drinks (and condoms). The public toilet just behind it is clean.

Children enjoy Patriarch's Pond

The Café Margarita where we will dine is just across the street on the opposite corner, but first we're going up to a couple of museums. Follow Bronnaya Malaya Ulitsa (Бронная Малая ул.) up past the Dutch A-Markt supermarket on the right and the French one on the left. Just next door is a small crafts shop where you may find some pretty nice hand-worked (they claim) table linen and traditional embroidery on felt. At the corner you'll see **Aist**, one of the original co-op restaurants. This is a handy place to remember because you don't need a reservation for lunch and it's open for coffee in the afternoon. At Aist, cross the road and cut down the path between the garden on your left and the building on your right. This will take you to the **Museum of Vandalism** on your left.

When I was a child, I always wondered what this neat but crumbling low-rise building was. When I was pacing out this itinerary, I was struck by a sign that looked like graffiti rather than a museum legend. It looked so new, it was barely dry. A make-shift pot stands precariously on the chair holding open the door – pop a few rubles in it as you enter.

If you're wearing good or light clothes, beware. The dust lies thick on everything except the works of sculptor and self-appointed curator Sergei Alexandrov. He explained he had been passing the place one day and saw the door open. When he looked inside, he realised this had been the studio of the sculptor Tomski, the darling of the Soviet regime. He decided to squat in the building and turn it into an impromptu museum. Busts of the 'heroes' of the Soviet Union are stacked around the walls, vying for space with death masks of Lenin. But there are some beautiful broken friezes depicting workers that may tempt you. Don't buy them – you wouldn't be able to export them. Sergei is a friendly

In the Museum of Vandalism

guy and willing to talk, though his four words of English may make communication difficult if you've no Russian.

The flowing art-nouveau lines of the **Gorky Museum** form a sharp contrast (it's just down the street on the corner Spiridoneyska (Спиридонéевский пер., formerly Alekseya Tolstogo). When Gorky returned to the Soviet Union in the early 1930s, the authorities presented him with this house (Aleksiy Tolstoy, grandson of the great Tolstoy, got the stables and outbuildings). Gorky had never liked the guy who commissioned the house – Stepan Riabushinsky of the prolific merchant dynasty of powerful 'capitalists'; his brother Nikolai was head of the Moscow Stock Exchange before 1917. Nor did Gorky like the house itself, which was designed both inside and out and built by one of the most creative architects of the day, Fedor Shekhtel.

Gorky Museum stair

Entry (through a side door on the left-hand side, not through the main entrance) is free, but you are expected to sign the book at the door. Don't miss the moulded ceiling designed to create a sub-aquatic atmosphere in the library, or the stained-glass windows lighting deep oriental carpets beneath the simply elegant dining chairs in the room next door. Drool over the marble staircase representing sea waves as you make your way upstairs (you may be allowed to take off your slippers for the climb; it's so slippery, you could break your neck – but what a way to go) to examine the last photographs of Gorky. These have never previously been shown publicly, and many Russians are now wondering how he could have surrounded himself with unsavoury types like Yagoda (head of the NKVD – forerunner of the KGB – and prime mover behind the Stalin purges).

When you leave the museum, you'll see a **church** (the Ascension) cloaked in scaffolding (restoration takes years in this city). Besides being a hot-bed of monarchist activity, this place has the best church choir in Moscow, so try and combine a visit with a service. Women should always cover their heads in Orthodox churches and no one should have their hands in their pockets.

Retrace your steps back to **Café Margarita**. They don't take reservations here, so it's first come, first served for rubles. They open at 6pm, so get there early (you may have to queue). The food is not exactly cuisine, but this is a city hot-spot and you may get a good casserole. The desserts are sweet and sticky and very good.

8. Russian Roulette

Racing and gambling at the Hippodrome. Dinner at the Delhi.

If you think riding the Metro has given you a reasonable insight into typical Muscovite behaviour, fashion, and faces, think again. The **Hippodrome** shows a side of Moscow rarely seen by tourists, who tend to stay in the centre. In spite of all that, the racing is professional, fast and thrilling. Racing days are Wednesday, Friday and Sunday. Make for Metro Begovaya (Беговая) and just follow the crowds (keep the railway tracks on your right and follow Begovaya Ulitsa round to the main entrance). The 19th-century Hippodrome, where the sport of tsars has been a popular outing for all classes since 1857, now doubles as the venue for the **Casino Royale**. Open on different days from the race-track, the casino relives the Hippodrome's illustrious past as currency-paying, evening-dressed patrons roll in to try

Exotic show at the Delhi

their luck at roulette (not the Russian kind) and black-jack.

You'll probably want a shower and a change of clothes before heading out for dinner, but the **Delhi** is only two stops towards the city centre on the same line as Begovaya. Get out at Krasnopresnenskaya (Краснопресненская), turn left out of the exit and walk up Krasnaya Presnya Ulitsa (Красная Пресня ул.) to 23b. The Delhi offers good old-fashioned Indian cuisine. Try the tandoori chicken – it's a house speciality. I've explained the idiosyncrasies of ruble/currency dining in the eating out section, but the Delhi is even more old-fashioned in this respect, retaining both a ruble room and a currency room. In the ruble room (Tel: 252 1766), you'll be treated to displays by illusionists, contortionists and fire-eaters. The currency room (Tel: 255 0492) is rather more sedate, and has been recently renovated – the floor show is 'exotic'.

The Hippodrome

Fresh air in the city

9. On the Waterside

Lazy afternoon on Moscow's strand. Dinner at Slavyansky Bazar.

Moscow has all the pollution problems of most big cities – and then some more. Although your immediate association with the Russian capital may be snow, it can get pretty hot and steamy in the summer time – anything up to 30°C (86°F) in July and August. If you're fed up with crowded streets, sticky people and frayed tempers, head out for **Serebryany Bor** (Серебряный Бор) which is the nearest thing to a beach in this land-locked city. Take a picnic along and your swimming gear. Pick up trolley-bus No 20 on Red Square; it will take you all the way.

There's some new housing there, but most of the 'forest' remains unspoilt. Throw down your towel on a grassy or sandy spot along the river, dig out your copy of *Gorky Park*, and settle down for a quiet afternoon. Alternatively you could hire a boat, or wander the tree-shaded paths. There is even a nudist section. If your stomach starts rumbling, one of the countless vendors will supply food and drink, but traditionally we eat *shashlik* and ice-cream at the beach.

Slavyansky Bazar

Head back to the city feeling rested, and maybe even bronzed, in readiness for dinner-dancing at **Slavyansky Bazar** (Nikolskaya Ulitsa/Никольская ул. 13; Tel: 921 1872 – rubles and currency – hell, I didn't know they'd started taking hard money). Unashamedly tacky now, this restaurant was once the haunt of the artistic crowd during the 19th-century revival of Russian folk arts (a movement that paralleled the English pre-Raphaelites and William Morris). The tradition of presenting 'authentic' Russian sword and folk dancing that started then has survived, though in a rather kitsch form. The main point here is that the restaurant survived the whole Soviet era. It remained a symbol of something that harked back to a different time and a different life; the food (now not up to much, though the *zakuski* can include caviar on better days) was always good and the vokda flowed as generously as nationalist sentiment.

10. Tour of Novodevichiy Convent

A religious house cum fortress; a once fashionable cemetery. Dinner at U Pirosmani.

Take the Metro southwest to Sportivnaya (Спортивная). Turn right at the exit and walk up to Usacheva Ulitsa (Усачёва ул.). Cross this street and turn left up Uchebniy pereulok (Учебный пер.). Once you get to the end of the street, if you look left, you'll see the Novodevichiy Convent walls – there are entrances in both the southern and northern walls (the former leads to the convent, the latter to the cemetery).

This grand walled convent in a loop of the River Moskva was built in the 16th century ostensibly as part of the chain of religious-houses-cum-fortresses that sur-

Novodevichiy Convent

rounded the old city. In fact, it was later used primarily as a dumping ground for inconvenient royal and *boyar* (noble) ladies (see *History and Culture*). This is perhaps one of the most beautiful of the city's surviving convents as it is not only well-preserved, but its site offers wonderful views over the river.

Founded by Grand Duke Basil III, father of Ivan the IV (the Formidable rather than the mistranslated Terrible), the complex with its 16 golden domes is now part of the **Russian Historical Museum**. The early tsars were convinced that after the fall of Constantinople, Moscow would become the 'third Rome'. They, and the Orthodox Church, saw the Russians as the true preservers of Christianity, and this notion is expressed in the main 16th-century fresco in Our Lady of Smolensk Cathedral.

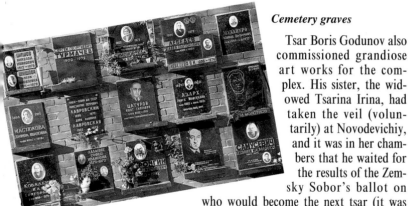

Tsar Boris Godunov also commissioned grandiose art works for the complex. His sister, the widowed Tsarina Irina, had taken the veil (voluntarily) at Novodevichiy, and it was in her chambers that he waited for the results of the Zemsky Sobor's ballot on who would become the next tsar (it was Boris G, of course). To show his gratitude, and possibly relief, he began restoration work and ordered new icons for the cathedral's iconostasis (icon screen). Ironically, the complex's next patron, Sofia, Peter the Great's half-sister, would later become its prisoner when she fell foul of the intrigues, power games and insecurities surrounding the early tsars and the succession. Sofia presented the five-tier iconostasis in the centre of the cathedral. Considered a masterpiece of pictorial art, it took three years (1683–86), and three artists, Andreyev, Mikhailov and Zinoviev, to create it — don't miss it.

Pop into the **Dormition Refectory Church** if only to hear the choir (times of services are posted at the gates) before having a look at the convent cells that were exactly that for a number of royal ladies. To take the veil was effectively the only form of 'divorce' allowed by the Orthodox Church.

The chambers where the women spent the rest of their days are in various buildings through the complex.

Before dinner, wander through the convent's **cemetery**. For centuries it was a fashionable place to be buried and Chekhov is here, along with composer Scryabin. Stalin's first wife, Nadezhda Alleleuva, lies beside pre-Revolutionary noble women, and Nikita Khrushchev also chose Novodevichiy as his final resting place.

Georgians are said to be the *bon vivants* of the former Soviet Union – the best

Be patient at U Pirosmani

wines and a great cuisine grew up in the sunny southern state. Located not far from the northern gates of the convent, **U Pirosmani** (Novodevichiy Proyezd/Новодевичий пр. 4, Tel: 247 1926; food for rubles, alcohol for currency) is the best of all the Georgian eateries in the city. You should try the traditional *hachapuri* (hot bread with melted cheese) and *lobio* (bean stew with chunks of meat) starters with spicy beef stew to follow. Service can be a bit slow: sit back and enjoy the breathtaking view over Novodevichiy.

1. Sergiev Posad and Abramtsevo

A visit to the monastery at Sergiev Posad (formerly Zagorsk), calling at a toy museum en route, and returning via Abramtsevo. If you would prefer to opt for an organised tour that will take in both Sergiev Posad and Abramtsevo, call TTC in Sergio Posad on Tel: 8254 26209. It will cost you currency, but it may turn out to be the easiest way to see both if you don't have a car. If you want to see the monastery's superb art collection, you have to arrange permission in advance, Tel: 8254 45356/ 45350.

Into the fields

Until not long ago foreigners had to have special permission to visit the monastery town of **Sergiev Posad** (still familiar as Zagorsk). It is 65km (40 miles) outside the city centre and foreigners were not allowed to travel more than 40km (25 miles) in any direction from the Kremlin. That has all changed now, and you can go where you like.

If you fancy driving, this is a good opportunity to rent a car. A great stretch of the highway to the old monastery town of Sergiev Posad was recently built by German engineers (we call it the 'German road') and it's smooth going all the way (take Mira Prospekt (Мира проспект) leading to the Yaroslavskoye Shosse (Ярославское шоссе) out of the city).

If you prefer to travel by train, take the Metro to Komsomol-

Symbols of Sergiev Posad – the monastery domes

skaya (Комсомольская) and pick up the *elektrichka* at **Yaroslavsky Voksal**. (The story goes that when the Russians were planning their first railway, a group of engineers went to London to study its suburban lines. They were taken to Vauxhall station, and the interpreter somehow conveyed the impression that stations were called Vauxhalls – the Russians adopted the word, and it's still used today.)

The station at Sergiev Posad is on the outskirts of the town, so it's a fair walk to the monastery (follow the domes). On the way, you'll see a beetroot-red building on your left. This is the **toy museum**. For centuries, Sergiev Posad was a centre of toy-making. The museum was established by a local businessman at the turn of the century (although the official guide book gives credit to the People's Commissariat for Education). It contains a collection of local and foreign-made playthings that will appeal to everyone. My personal favourites are the wax-faced dolls and 19th-century wooden toys in the first room on your right on the ground floor.

Next door to the museum is a reasonable café/restaurant for refreshment. In the town itself you could have lunch or dinner at the

Orthodox offering

Soviet-style restaurant on the main square (it's just across the car park from the monastery gates). Or try the **Zagorsk Hotel** just up the road.

When entering the monastery, be prepared to run the gauntlet of old people begging under the arched main gate. I usually bring a lot of change with me because I can't bear the sight of elderly folk in need. You'll see that many women wear a scarf or hat. Although not obligatory in the grounds, some kind of head-covering for women is essential inside the churches.

The history of Sergiev Posad is interwoven with that of the tsars. Established in the mid-14th century when St Sergius made a small clearing in the dense forest that surrounded Moscow, its first royal visitor was Prince Dmitry Donskoy. He arrived in 1380 to ask Sergius for his blessing on the Russian war against the Tartars. Dmitry went on to beat the nation's long-time enemies for the first time at the Battle of Kulikovo. The holy man's benediction was considered a real contribution to the victory and his prestige grew phenomenally.

Sergiev Posad became the centre of learning for the whole of the Duchy of Muscovy. The saint's disciples wandered to the farthest corners of the country and established over 150 monasteries. Sergius himself was a great scholar and set up the first written chronicles of Russia – he also founded one of the finest libraries in the country.

It was in Sergiev Posad that another Prince Dmitry sought divine help in driving out Russia's enemies. In 1611 the monastery itself was besieged by 30,000 Poles. After 16 months the Poles gave up and headed back to Moscow, where they were occupying the Kremlin. Afterwards, the monastery became the centre of national resistance. When Prince Dmitry and Kuzma Minin finally managed to raise an army to expel the Poles, the monastery's gold was used to pay for equipment and horses. Following the victory Mikhail Romanov was elected tsar and he became the monastery's patron.

The monastery managed to survive throughout the Soviet era, although it was badly in need of restoration and renovation. Over the past few years, work has been ongoing and it has regained some of its original splendour. As you enter the main gate, the building directly in front of you is the **Holy Spirit cathedral** (entrance is on the far side). Just outside the doors is a small, gingerbread house sheltering a well for holy water. Legend has it that the well sprang up during the Polish siege. Tsar Boris Godunov, his wife and two children are buried just behind it.

St Sergius's remains lie encased in a silver shrine in the **Church of the Holy Trinity** at the far right of the main courtyard. The sole illumination in the church is provided by rows and rows of icon lamps in precious and base metals which were donated by grateful Russian supplicants; the type of metal reflected the individual's wealth and status.

The monastery is also home to one of the most remarkable collections of religious, secular and applied arts ranging from the 14th to the 20th century. Unfortunately, visitors need advance permission before they can view the amazing vestments hand-embroidered in gold thread, the medieval icons, translucent porcelain and other treasures. The introduction to this itinerary explains how you can arrange a visit.

It's a curious experience to wander here, especially on weekdays when the monks often outnumber the visitors. For many Russians, it is like walking back into the past, as

After church

Abramtsevo Dacha

though the Soviet era never happened. Tea and a proletarian bun at the café across the square brings you back to reality with a bump.

Travel back in time once again by taking the road (or *elektrichka*) back towards Moscow and exiting at the turn-off for **Abramtsevo** (daily 10am–5pm; last tickets are sold at 4.20pm).

Railway tycoon Mamantov's singular **dacha** on the edge of the village became the heart of the 19th-century Russian cultural revival. Mamantov purposely chose a small, traditional wooden cottage rather than a more elaborate palatial building. The general consensus at the time was that Russian mores and arts had been swamped by French culture. The revival of Russian arts produced a whole new movement in the closing decades of the last century. Everybody who was anybody in the arts world went to Abramtsevo. Nikolai Gogol read the first chapters of *Dead Souls* to a select audience here, which included Ivan Turgenev and actor Mikhail Shchepkin.

The original small wooden *dacha* was enlarged and improved by Mamantov and he commissioned a number of other buildings as well as a beautiful Japanese-style water garden. The overgrown gardens still retain much of their natural beauty. The old traditional craft of ceramic tile-making was reintroduced here in the 1880s and the results decorate the tiny church in the grounds.

2. Klyazmenskoye Reservoir

Once the preserve of ranking *apparatchiks*, the **Burevestnik Yacht Club** has now opened its jetties to anyone who fancies taking to water on the **Klyazmenskoye Reservoir**. To get there, catch the *elektrichka* from Savyolovsky Voksal to Khlebnikovo (journey is around 30 minutes), or exit the Dmitrovskoye Shosse (Дмитровское шоссе) at the 27 km post.

Calm waters

Your best bet is to phone in advance and explain what you want. The club has boats and windsurfers for hire, but you might prefer to take one of the day-trips they organise on small yachts. The restaurant is adequate, but you can take a picnic lunch along. Tel: 131 8345 or 229 2573 for details.

Right, the monastery, Sergiev Posad

Shopping

Contrary to popular images of Russia and her capital, long queues outside shops have just about disappeared. The reason is that the introduction of the 'free market' and the withdrawal of state subsidies on staple goods has turned shopping into a kind of free-for-all. Vendors hawk the oddest collections of wares on just about every street corner, and normal groceries are equally, and sometimes prohibitively, expensive wherever you go.

If you're looking for bargains, you'll probably be disappointed. Even in Soviet times, quality goods were expensive, and that hasn't changed. But the explosion of street-sellers and kiosks means you can sometimes pick up caviar, good vodka and other classy items for very reasonable prices. Traditional souvenirs – lacquer work, Lithuanian amber and hand-carved woodwork, for instance – are also pretty pricey; your best bet for these is **Izmaylovsky Park** on weekends (*see Morning Itinerary 4*). The same applies to Russian fur hats. Supplies are unreliable, so I can't guarantee the stores listed below will always have what they are supposed to stock. All the shops listed here are Russian, ruble stores (I haven't included the currency establishments as these tend to stock the kind of Western goods on sale in most European high streets, though often a year out of date).

A word of warning here: don't buy antiques or old paintings, icons or samovars at markets. To export items like these, you'll need official papers, and these can only be supplied by registered shops and galleries. A visiting American academic didn't believe me when I told him this – his three beautiful samovars are still locked up somewhere in the nether regions of the customs area at Sheremetyevo II.

Izmaylovsky market

Department Stores

DETSKY MIR (Children's World)
Okhotny Ryad 2
Monday to Saturday 8am–9pm
The biggest store for kids' stuff in the city, you can (usually) buy everything here from buggies and blow-up toys, to sporting equipment and colouring books. The giant cuckoo clock dominating the cavernous main hall starts whirring and moving on the hour – worth a visit just to see this. Can get very crowded.

MAGAZIN MALYSH (Little One's Store)
Kutuzovsky Prospekt 8
Monday to Saturday 10am–8pm
The best place to find warm, flannel baby clothes and neat blankets. The baby rattles and play-things (often quality wooden items) make good gifts for kids.

TSUM (Central Department Store)
Ulitsa Petrovka 2
Monday to Saturday 8am–9pm
There's a growing trend towards small co-operative boutiques inside Moscow's second-most famous store. The move into free enterprise means you may find good amber or coral jewellery, Central Asian rugs, furs, and samovars alongside an amazing range of kitsch.

Boutique in GUM

GUM (State Department Store)
Krasnaya Ploshchad 3 (Red Square)
Monday to Saturday 8am–9pm
Primarily household goods – linen

and such. But you should pop into this store just to admire the fabulous pastel interior.

The Voentorg – worth checking out

VOENTORG (Military Goods Store)
Noviy Arbat 10
Monday to Saturday 8am–9pm
Ostensibly the place where Red Army officers got their kit. The store also stocks a bizarre range of weird and wonderful goods, from kitchen storage jars (with Cyrillic-script labelling) to kids' watches and fishing equipment. Worth checking out – you never know what you may find.

Specialist Shops

FUR KOMMISSIONI
Pushkinskaya Ulitsa 30
Monday to Saturday 9am–8pm; lunch break 2pm–3pm
However strong the anti-fur lobby may be in the West, every time I head towards Europe friends beg me to bring hats, jackets, gloves, muffs. This store is well-stocked and actually has a wide range of sizes. Look out for astrakhan coats. Be warned – it's expensive.

UNISAT
Ulitsa Vakhtangova 5
Monday to Saturday 11am–8pm; Sunday 11am–7pm
Porcelain, icons, art-deco antiques and real silverware – if you buy here, make sure you get the paperwork so you can take your treasure out of the country.

Amber necklaces at Yantar

KOMMISSIONI
Ulitsa Tverskaya Yamskaya 16
Monday to Friday 10am–7pm, Saturday 10am–8pm; lunch break 2–3pm
Good quality clothes and porcelain here, but make straight for the crystal counter – the goods are classy and reasonably priced.

ART SALON
Kutuzovsky Prospekt 26
Tuesday to Saturday 10am–7pm; lunch break 2–3pm
An artist's paradise. You can pick up pastels in elegant wooden boxes, clay modelling tools and everything else you need to produce that masterpiece. Many of the items on sale make good gifts.

Souvenir Shops
RUSSKIYE SOUVENIRY
Kutuzovsky Prospekt 9
Monday to Saturday 11am–8pm
Silverware, Central-Asian outfits, knitted socks, mittens and scarves, wonderful lacquer boxes and other interesting items.

YANTAR
Gruzinsky Val 14
Monday to Saturday 10am–7pm, lunch break 2–3pm
The shop's name means amber, and that is exactly what it sells. The real thing here, imported directly from Lithuania.

Fashion Stores
DOM MODY – (Zaitsev Showroom)
Prospekt Mira 21
Monday to Saturday 10am–7pm, lunch break 1.30–2.15pm
Zaitsev's creations are well made and stylish, but his winter coats are out of this world. You'll have to pay a fee to get in, but it's worth it.

DOM MODY
Smolensky Bulvar (at the Smolenskaya-Filevskaya Metro station)
Monday to Saturday 10am–7pm, lunch break 1–2pm
Rather more down-market Soviet designer fashion, but you may find a well-cut frock or coat here. Browsing through stores like this will give you

Matryoschka dolls

some idea of what is on offer for the ordinary Muscovite woman-in-the-street.

TROIKA
Ulitsa Bolshaya Polyanka 3
Monday to Friday 10am–7pm; Saturday 10am–6pm; lunch break 2–3pm
Warm, fur-lined boots for both adults and children.

Food Shops/Markets

The so-called 'farmers' markets' have long been a way of life in Moscow. These were the places where you bought special items when you had guests coming for dinner. Inflation has sent already high prices through the roof, but they're still as popular as ever. The best are the Tsentralny on Tsvetnoi Bulvar 15 and Cheryomushkinsky Rynok on Lomonosovsky Prospekt 1.

Gastronoom No 20
Ulitsa Bolshaya Lubyanka 14
Monday to Saturday 8am–9pm, Sunday 8am–7pm
Nicknamed the KGB gastronoom, it was always well-stocked and miraculously still is. A great chocolate counter and champagne are the main attractions – don't buy the fish.

Emergency Food Supplies

Although getting a table in a restaurant is easier than it used to be, you may still end up hungry and with no place to go. Your best bet in this case is to go to one of the currency supermarkets, where you can buy the kind of goodies available at home.

Stockmann
Zatsepsky Val 4/8
Monday to Sunday 10am–8pm
Stocks the full range of Western supermarket items, including cheeses, salamis, fresh fruit, bottled water and alcohol. (Credit cards only.)

Tsentralny farmers' market

Art market on the Arbat

A-Markt
Malaya Bronnaya Ulitsa 27/14
Monday to Sunday 10am–8pm
Dutch joint venture with good range of cheeses and other picnic goodies. (Hard currency only.)

Intercar
Peking Hotel, Bolshaya Sadovaya 5/1
Monday to Friday 10am–8pm, Saturday and Sunday 11am–7pm
Prices are given in Deutschmarks at this German joint venture. Pick up bread, *wurst* and cheeses here. (Hard currency only.)

Tino Fontana
Mezhdunarodnaya Hotel, Krasnopresnenskaya Nab. 12
Monday to Saturday 10am–7pm, Sunday 10am–2pm
Italian delicatessen stock including good selection of national wines (hard currency only).

The Bakery
Penta Hotel, Olympisky Prospekt 18/1
Monday to Sunday 7am–10pm
Off the beaten track, but worth knowing about. Freshly baked bread and pastries from 7am every day, including Sunday!

Eating Out

Over 70 years of institutionalised food earned Soviet cooking a bad name, but Russian *haute cuisine* has simply been biding its time to re-emerge in the form of feather-light blinies and caviar, *borscht*, Russian salads, smoked fish starters, mushroom or lamb *juliennes* and other delicacies traditionally associated with pre-Revolutionary excesses. Today Moscow has its fair share of good and even very good restaurants – the problem now is getting a table.

The custom here is to reserve your table on the morning of the day you want to eat. It's a waste of time trying to do it in advance as the *maitre d'* will tell you to call back on the day, even if he has no reservation on his books. Once you've got him to admit that he may have a table for you, you will probably be asked in what currency you will be paying (although not always). If you say rubles, chances are there will be an indigestible silence at the other end, and you may be told that the ruble tables have all been reserved. If you speak Russian, argue the toss. If you don't, bow to the notion of actually getting something decent to eat and pay currency.

The main courses tend to be comparatively cheap; the money is made on the starters or *za-kuski*, so when you book you should specify a *chisti stol* (literally a clean table), or you will arrive to find a mass of *hors d'oeuvres* you don't want already waiting for you.

At some restaurants you should take your own alcoholic drinks as these may not be available, or you may not like their sickly sweet champagne or wine which I've noted. Table turnover is almost non-existent, so service is usually slow at most of the Russian (former Soviet) places. The list below is almost exhaustive because there aren't that many eateries.

Reserve your table first

ast food

AIST
Malaya Bronnaya 1/8
Tel: 291 6692
Rubles
Serves Georgian and other ethnic food, including *plov* and dumplings, at this candle-lit, rather tacky eatery. One of the first co-op restaurants, it's still a popular hang-out especially for yuppie Muscovites. No reservations needed for lunch.

ARAGVI
Ulitsa Tverskaya 6
Tel: 229 8506
Rubles
State-owned but excellent restaurant. The chicken *satsivi* (baked in a walnut and coriander sauce) will make your mouth water. They usually have inexhaustible supplies of dry champagne and wines.

ARKADIA
3 Teatralny Proyezd
Tel: 926 9008
Rubles
A fairly new addition, this is a great place to drink good Georgian wines in a typically Russian atmosphere. Try their bliny with caviar and take wads of rubles along for the bill.

ARLECCHINO
Druzhinnikoskaya Ulitsa 15
Tel: 205 7088
Major credit cards only
Expensive and not always as good as it should be – all ingredients are either flown or trucked in from Italy.

But the ambience is upmarket and the wines Italian, so if you've had enough of mayonnaised salads, and long for a risotto, this is the place. Your credit card will have to be very flexible to handle the bill.

ATRIUM
Leninsky Prospekt 44
Tel: 137 3008
Major credit cards only
Stylish and not overly expensive. Its atrium offers a fixed menu featuring Russian nouvelle cuisine. A personal favourite of mine.

BOYARSKY
Metropol Hotel (fourth floor),
Teatralny Proyezd 1/4
Tel: 927 6089
Super pricey, but the traditional Russian cuisine is equally super. Caviar-stuffed trout is just one of the dishes you can eat with pre-Revolutionary table silver. Don't bother with Le Bistro, the Metropol's other eatery.

Zakuski or starters

CHAMPS ELYSÉES
Pullman Hotel, Korovinskoye Chausse 10
Tel: 488 8000
Hard currency
The fabulous French food is well worth the trek. Expect a hefty bill.

DANILOVSKY
Bolshoi Starodanilovsky Pereulok 5
Tel: 954 0566
Rubles or hard currency
Located in the bunker-like hotel next

door to the monastery. It's said that the guys guarding the gate are former KGB and I can well believe it, but the food is great and the home-made ice cream a real dream. Very pricey, but worth it.

DRUZHBA
Expocentre, Krasnopresnenskaya nab.12
Tel: 255 2970
Rubles or credit cards
Lavish displays of caviar and fresh salads add to the atmosphere of opulence at this small co-op restaurant that doubles as an art gallery. Everything is good here, but the suckling pig is excellent.

FARKHAD
Bolshaya Marfinskaya 4
Tel: 218 4136
Rubles and hard currency
Bring your own wine to this exotic Azerbaijani eatery where the food is beautifully prepared. As a main course, try the *shashliks* (meat on skewers) and *dolmas*.

GURIA
Komsomolski Prospekt 7
Tel: 246 0378
Rubles
Not exactly upmarket, but this Georgian co-op is one of the few places in town where you can walk in off the street without a lunch or early dinner reservation. The *hachapuri* (hot bread and melted cheese) is fabulous.

IN VINO
Ukraina Hotel, Kutuzovsky Prospekt 2/1
Tel: 243 2316
Hard currency
Extremely expensive, but the view over the River Moskva makes it worth the money. The menu is limited and the standards not always consistent, but go for the fried scampi or beef and you can't go wrong.

KARINA
Solyansky Proyezd 1–3
Tel: 924 0369
Rubles
Exquisite traditional Russian cuisine. The ambience is quiet and almost stylish. Try any one of the wide range of soups as a starter or opt for the amazing mushrooms in sour cream. Main courses are anything but run-of-the-mill, but go for the cognac-marinated lamb – it's delicious.

KOLKHIDA
Stroyenie (building) 2, Sadovo-Samotechnaya 6
Tel: 299 6757
Rubles
Another of the Georgian jewels. Bring your own wine to go with the mutton and *dolmas*. If you want to sample the *khinkali* (huge, juicy dumplings), arrange it in advance.

Kropotkinskaya 36, a co-op restaur

KROPOTKINSKAYA 36
Ulitsa Prechistenka 36
Tel: 201 7500
Hard currency and credit cards
The first, and still the best co-op restaurant. The stuffed carp is sensational. They make their own ice cream.

MEI-HUA
Stroyenie 1, Ulitsa Rusakovskaya 2/1
Tel: 264 9574
Rubles and hard currency
A great Chinese restaurant right next door to the Rusalka Café. (There's no

El Rincon Espanol

sign and the doorbell is half hidden). Exquisite food; pork with peanuts is especially recommended.

RAZGULYAI
Ulitsa Spartakovskaya 11
Tel: 267 7613
Rubles and hard currency
A cellar eatery where the traditional Russian cuisine is simple but consistently good. A gypsy band plays here at the weekends.

EL RINCON ESPANOL
Okhotny Ryad 7
Tel: 292 2893
Hard currency
It seems odd to enjoy *tapas* and sangria on the ground floor of the Stalinist Moskva Hotel, but maybe that's no more than a sign of the times. Try the paella.

RUSALOCHKA
Smolensky Bulvar 12
Tel: 248 4438
Hard currency
A Danish venture. The seafood dishes have to be seen to be believed.

SKAZKA
Tovarishchevsky Pereulok 1
Tel: 271 0998
Rubles and major credit cards
Its name means fairy-tale and the decor adds to the illusion that you've stepped into something from Hans Christian Andersen. The *zakuski* are recommended, as are the *bliny* and caviar if they're available.

Villa Peredelkino, restaurant in a dacha

STANISLAVSKOGO 2
Ulitsa Stanislavskogo 2
Tel: 291 8689
Rubles
Affectionately known as Emily's after the owner, this is one of my favourites. The food is wonderful, the ambience elegant, and the music (violin and piano) classical. Emily will only take bookings on the day after 6pm, and she's very choosy – if you speak no Russian, try French. This is a great place to combine with a Wednesday recital at the Stanislavsky Museum just down the street.

TAGANKA CAFE
Zemlyanoi Val 76
Tel: 272-7320
Rubles and hard currency
A popular lunch and dinner spot for actors from the Taganka Theatre nearby, the first-floor restaurant offers some of the best *pelmeni* (meat-filled ravioli) in the city.

VILLA PEREDELKINO
Peredelkino Village
Tel: 435-1478
Major credit cards only
Don't go for the mediocre pseudo-Italian food. This was once the *dacha* of Brezhnev's daughter and its main attractions are that it provides an interesting insight into how the wealthy used to live, and that it is in the former writers' colony of Peredelkino. All the 19th and early 20th century artistic greats had their *dachas* here. Don't bother with the Russian dishes. Last *elektrichka* back to Moscow leaves around half past midnight.

Nightlife

Until very recently, nightlife in Moscow consisted almost exclusively of classical concerts, ballet, theatre and opera performances, cinema, or an evening at a dinner-dance, where the vodka flowed and people expected to stay until they were turfed out by the staff. Restaurants at the big hotels were the usual venues for private parties, and foreigners were a rare sight. Pubs and bars where people would simply hang out before or after dinner disappeared in the 1930s. The typical tourist places, such as the Slavyansky Bazar and Nasional Hotel restaurant, were exceptions, as were the bars in the major tourist hotels. As glasnost took hold of the

Nightlife is back in Moscow – but it can be sleazy

city and co-ops sprang up, we began to enjoy the type of nightlife that our grandparents had taken for granted and we knew nothing about – popular concerts, open-air gigs and alternative eateries where young people read anti-establishment poetry, sang 'subversive' songs, and generally had a good time.

Efforts to restore popular culture are at an interim stage, with most venues charging currency. For most Muscovites the range of nightlife on offer now is still beyond their pockets. Because most of the nightlife is geared to Westerners with currency (and these are often men in the city on business), or wealthy Russians, it tends to

be sleazy and expensive. Muscovites usually opt for a dinner arrangement if they have something to celebrate (see *Eating Out*).

One of the best and least sleazy venues for late-night dancing is **Stas Namen's Victoria** (rubles or credit cards), aka Hard Rock Café, deep in Gorky Park (Zelyoni Theatre, Gorky Park; Tel: 237 0709), but you have to be able to handle the decibels. Get there late as the place only starts hotting up after 10pm (don't wander about in the park alone).

Peter's Place (currency) on Zemlyanoi Val 72 (Tel: 298 3248) if you're up for wall-to-wall striptease.

The current hotspot is the **Red Zone** (Leningradsky Prospekt 39) where the decor is borrowed from Gulag camps: topless go-go dancers who shuffle around wicker cages suspended from the ceiling. Ten dollars or 1,600 rubles will gain you entrance to this loud, popular club. Women are admitted free, so it's a paradise for middle-aged businessmen on the look out for 'company'.

The **Moscow Hill** (10pm–5am) is the latest addition to the circuit. The entrance fee is $15 (for both sexes), but includes a free drink. Men will have to prove they are over 30 and women that they are over 21.

The same age restrictions apply to men at **Night Flight**, where dress code is rigidly enforced: don't bother coming in a suit, tie and sneakers, you'll be sent home to change your shoes. Again the $15 admission includes a free drink. Music is good, but the crowd is again predominantly middle-aged men and very young girls.

On the bar scene, all the joint-venture hotels have one and some have three or four. Most are interchangeable and you'll meet the same crowd (foreign businesspeople, correspondents, etc) at all of them. The bars in **Intourist**, **Cosmos** and the **Mezh** vie for the title of 'sleaziest in town', but it appears that lots of people like them that way, as they're always jam-packed.

On a more genteel note, **The Savoy Club** at the Tumba Golf Club (Ulitsa Dovzhenko 1; Tel: 147 7368) is very upmarket and elegant; the **Tren-Mos Bar** (Ostozhenka Ulitsa 1/9; Tel: 202 5722) is a small, intimate venue where US ex-pats congregate; the **Medusa** on the boat *MS Alexander Blok* (Krasnopresnenskaya Nab. 12; Tel: 255 9284) is pretty sleazy, but fun. The **Galaxy** (Selskokhozyaistvenny Pereulok 2, near the Cosmos Hotel; Tel: 181 2074) is a pub-style bar where the black-market crowd practises darts and knocks back English beer. My personal favourite is **El Rincon Espanol** (Tel: 292 2893) on the ground floor of the Moskva Hotel on Okhotny Ryad, where you can prop up the bar until late.

Casinos

Muscovites have always enjoyed a flutter, although **casinos** were considered products of Western decadence in the Soviet era. We seem to be making up for lost time because more than a dozen have opened within the last couple of years. Dress codes are enforced. You can have a drink and just watch the action – you're not obliged to gamble – in a comfortable ambience until 4am. Cover charges are $10–$15 unless otherwise indicated. The best are:

ALEXANDER BLOK (no cover charge)
Krasnopresnenskaya Nab (opposite the Mezh), Tel: 255 9323

ARBAT
Noviy Arbat 21, Tel: 291 1172

BOMBAY
Rublyovskoye Shosse 91, Tel: 141 5504

CLUB FORTUNA (no cover charge)
Mezh Hotel, Krasnopresnenskaya Nab. 12, 2nd Floor, Tel: 252 3440

MOSCOW
Leningradskaya Hotel, Ulitsa Kalanchovskaya 21/40, Tel: 975 1967

CASINO ROYALE
Begovaya 22, Tel: 945 1410

At the Bolshoi

SAVOY CLUB
Savoy Hotel, Rozhdestvenka Ulitsa 3, Tel: 929 8630

TARS
Ukraine Hotel, Kutuzovsky Prospekt 2/1, Tel: 243 3011

Concerts, Opera and Ballet

The city has numerous venues for classical concerts, opera and ballet – pick up a copy of *The Moscow Times* for full details. The main halls are:

Ballet & Opera
THE BOLSHOI THEATRE
Teatralnaya Ploshchad
Box office: 292 9986
Most performances begin at 7pm; matinées at 12 noon. (The Bolshoi is usually closed in July and August.)

PEOPLE'S FRIENDSHIP THEATRE
Tverskoi Bulvar 23
Box office: 203 8582
Often features modern dance. Check out the programme posted at the door.

Classical
TCHAIKOVSKY CONSERVATORY (Great and Lesser Halls)
Ulitsa Gertsena 13
Box office: 299 3602
Concerts begin at 7.30pm.

Some bars open late

Puppet Theatre performance

TCHAIKOVSKY CONCERT HALL
Triumphalnaya Ploshchad
Box office: 299 6446
Concerts begin at 7.30pm.

Jazz

COTTON CLUB
Tel: 201 7067
The club's venue is a riverboat docked at Kievsky Vokzal pier. Sets begin at 7.30 and 10.30pm, and the boat departs at 8 and 11pm for a cruise down the river. Food and drinks for rubles.

Other Venues

If your Russian is good enough to handle theatre, check the papers for programmes. For non-Russian speakers, the following venues usually have performances that require no language skills. Programmes are posted outside; tickets are available from the venues' box offices and at kiosks in Metro stations.

CENTRAL PUPPET THEATRE
Sadovaya-Samotechnaya Ulitsa 3
Performances here appeal to all ages.

MOSCOW CIRCUS
Tzvetnoiy Bulvar 13 and Prospekt Vernadskogo 7
Famous throughout the world, the company performs at both venues, but I much prefer the original hall on Tzvetnoiy. It has been renovated recently but retains all the big-top magic of yesteryear; the newer venue is rather cavernous and less atmospheric.

OPERETTA THEATRE
Pushkinskaya Ulitsa 7
The name says it all.

ROSSIYA CONCERT HALL
Moskvoretskaya Nab. 1
A mixed bag of shows staged here — anything from techno-pop concerts to theatre performances.

The Moscow Circus performs at two venues

GETTING THERE

Moscow's international airport, Sheremetyevo II, is served by more than 30 international airlines, and is the major gateway to the country. Sheremetyevo is accordingly rather overcrowded, and formalities can take time (see *Visas and Customs* below for more details).

You can reach Moscow by rail, but it would take you about three days from Western Europe. The most popular rail route for international traffic is Helsinki to Moscow, arriving at St Petersburg Station. The Trans Siberian Express leaves from Yaroslavl Station.

Anyone intending to visit Moscow by

car should first contact Intourist, for recommended routes; there are only a few recognised overland entry points.

TRAVEL ESSENTIALS

Visas and Customs

Getting a visa for Russia is practically impossible for an individual traveller who doesn't want to book a package deal through a travel agent, or isn't visiting as the guest of a recognised Russian company/organisation or a private Russian citizen. This is partly a matter of tit for tat. Western countries are sparing with their visa allocations to Russian citizens because they are afraid of mass emigration. In their turn, the Russian authorities make life miserable for those wanting to travel east. There is also a very practical impediment – the lack of hotel beds. Russian embassies therefore stipulate that you have to have a definite place to stay before arrival.

If you are determined to organise your own trip, to apply for a visa you need a letter of invitation from a *bona fide* Russian organisation or company, or from an individual, which states categorically that you will be accommodated and looked after during your stay. The best thing to do is to run through your address book and find someone with some link to Russia and see if they can help

A welcome a-waiting

you organise an invitation. These people don't necessarily have to put you up, but finding a place is going to be difficult. A growing number of agencies can arrange for you to rent a Muscovite's apartment for the duration of your stay – for currency, of course (see *Where to Stay*). If all this proves impossible, opt for a package.

On the plane you'll be issued with two customs declaration forms. Fill in one with your name, etc (never leave blank spaces). You'll be asked what kind of currency you have and how much; list everything you have, even small change. On the reverse of the form list any valuables, ie portable computers, radios and their serial numbers, and even your wedding ring. If you're wise, you'll leave most of your expensive durables at home. You can bring any amount of currency into the country, but you must not import rubles.

When you land at Sheremetyevo, you first go through immigration. This takes so long that baggage reclaim is usually fairly swift.

Now for customs. Keep your declaration and your passport handy, and get ready to experience your first real encounter with ex-Soviet officialdom (the name has changed, but the people behind the desks are the same). Remain polite, try to smile winningly, and don't get angry – it gets you nowhere in this country. Don't lose your stamped declaration form – they won't let you out without it.

Finding a ride into town will be your first experience of the idiosyncrasies of economics in the city. If you can't afford the outrageous prices demanded by taxi-drivers or gypsy cabs, you can pick up a bus (number 551) outside the departure hall to Metro station Rechnoy Vokzal (Речной Вокзал) at the end of the green line; this will take you right into the city centre. Alternatively, if you have a hotel reservation at one of the big hotels, you can pick up the bus that ferries their guests to and fro.

If you travel by train, expect a three to four hour wait at the border when immigration and customs officials will pass through each and every compartment and unpack any suitcase they don't like. Again, patience is the virtue you're going to need most.

On departure, you should fill out your second customs declaration. It's a good idea to do this before you leave your hotel. Hand both (ie the stamped arrival one and the new one) to the customs official along with your passport before checking in.

Wrap up well in winter

Clothing and Climate

The traditional street image of Moscow is grey waves of fur-hatted, booted citizens struggling through deep snow. It is only accurate for less than half the year. Moscow has what is known as a 'land climate', which means it is warm in spring (April/May: 18°C/64°F), often hot in summer (June–August: 20–30°C/68–86°F), mild in autumn (September/October: 10–15°C/50–60°F) and freezing (anything down to minus 30°C/-22°F) for the rest of the year. If you come from anywhere outside the world's tropical zones, you don't have to plan a special wardrobe for spring through to autumn, although you are advised to bring either a raincoat or umbrella. A trip in winter means thermal underwear, warm headgear (also for men), and fleece-lined boots along with a sturdy, lined winter overcoat. *Babushkas* (elderly ladies) will shout and point at you if your head is not adequately covered in winter.

Cheap energy has meant homes, offices,

public buildings and stores are heated to around 23°C (73°F) in winter, and Muscovites therefore tend to wear light clothes under their outdoor winter coats.

Although the basic street scene appears rather drab, the Muscovites go in for some pretty fancy dressing – especially the ladies. Don't go to a good restaurant or to the theatre/opera in jeans. Eating out or a major Bolshoi performance are occasions to dress up. Other than that, anything goes.

Orthodox priests

Time

Moscow runs on Moscow Time and is three hours ahead of London, two hours ahead of European countries on CET, eight hours ahead of New York, and five hours behind Tokyo.

GETTING ACQUAINTED

Topography

Until the Revolution, Moscow was more or less divided into quarters. The arrival of the MosSoviet (the official city administration) after 1917 changed all that. The city was broken down into 10 districts, all run by a council.

Besides familiar landmarks such as the Kremlin, Pushkin Square and the Arbat, the main orientation points in the city are the Boulevard Ring, the Garden Ring and the Koltzevaya Avtodoroga (which translates literally as Ring Road). The Boulevard Ring and Garden Ring actually run along what used to be the old city walls and are clearly marked on all city maps.

These roads were built as part of the 20th-century remodelling of Moscow as the capital of Socialism. The basic idea was to create workers' suburbs outside the old centre (which is dominated by the Kremlin, and the old pre-Revolutionary Arbat, Zamosc-Vorechje (across the river from the Kremlin) and Kitai-Gorod (adjoining Red Square) quarters). A fast and reliable Metro network was built to ferry people to and from their places of work. If you look at a city plan, you'll see that the overground infrastructure is actually designed as a series of ringroads accessed by major arterial highways. Their construction sliced through old neighbourhoods, destroying many 19th-century areas, and new strings of uninspired tower blocks were erected in their place. As a result, Muscovites rarely talk about coming from this or that area, and don't divide the city into distinct quarters. Maybe that will all change now.

Religion

Religion, declared the 'opium of the people' by Karl Marx, is now playing an increasingly important role in people's lives. Under Gorbachev many churches were reopened for worship. Most Russian Orthodox Churches have a morning Divine Liturgy at 10am and an evening service at 6pm. Women should cover their heads in churches; mini-skirts and shorts tend to offend. If you wish to take photographs, ask first.

MONEY MATTERS

The ruble is the official currency of Russia. It breaks down into 100 *kopeks*. Coins come in one, two, three, five, 10, 15, 20 *kopeks* – but these are practically redundant because inflation has made them almost worthless. A new one-ruble coin is currently replacing the old note; paper denominations are three, five, 10, 25, 50, 100, 200, 500, 1,000 and 5,000.

Since the introduction of the 'market economy', you can pay for almost anything in just about any currency Russians can recognise as 'hard', Western money (pounds, marks, francs (French or Swiss), guilders, lira). But dollars are preferred. Your best bet is probably to change your

The Metro is famously grand

own currency into dollars before you arrive in Moscow as you may have trouble changing less familiar money – the official exchange office at the airport will accept only dollars in return for rubles.

All Russian banks will change your currency – the rate fluctuates madly and is currently anywhere between 400 and 440 rubles to the dollar. Crowds of disreputable-looking types hover around bank entrances offering much better rates. If you decide to do business with them, have the amount you want to change ready – don't display all your holiday money, credit cards, etc. And don't be too polite to re-count what you are given.

If you don't want to get involved in such encounters, go to a bank in one of the major hotels, or to one of the American Express offices at Sadovo-Kudrinskaya 21a or Noviy Arbat 32 where you can also change AmEx traveller's cheques into dollars (for a pretty large commission). If you do this, and are planning to leave the country with more dollars than you had when you arrived, you should ask for a *spravka* – the official exchange document – and keep it with your customs declaration form.

For a small fee, the Dialog Bank in the Radisson Hotel lobby offers a wire service to transfer money from your home bank. Tel: 941 8434/8349.

Major credit cards (AmEx, Mastercard, Visa, JB, Diner's Club) are very acceptable – even for a $2-dollar cup of coffee – and often more convenient than carrying cash.

Tipping

Even in Soviet times, people tipped waiters, cab-drivers, etc. However, there is no formal etiquette on how much. Leave what you think a service is worth. If you pay by credit card, don't put the tip on your card because the waiter won't get it.

GETTING AROUND

Metro

The Moscow Metro system is famous for its beauty – dazzling ceiling frescoes, crystal chandeliers, handsome marble halls and stained-glass panels. However, despite its splendour, it was designed to be fast, reliable and cheap, and miracu-

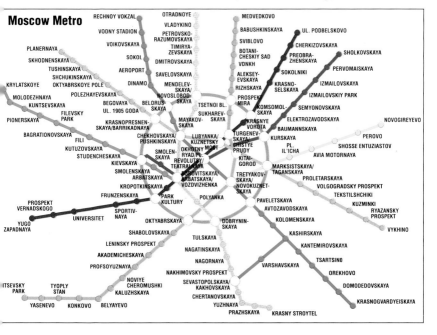

lously it still is. It is the best way to travel in Moscow. The fare is (currently) 3 rubles for any journey – buy tokens from ticket windows in the entry halls or try to get a monthly pass from vendors who usually sit close to main entrances.

Each station, even those at the same location, but on different lines, has a name of its own. For example Puschkinskaya, Tverskaya and Chekovskaya are given as individual stations even though they are interlinked. Each line has a name and these are used as orientation points, so check which line you need and memorise the Cyrillic words for it. There are two kinds of indicator boards in a station: one gives exits and transfer information and the other shows stations on the line.

Cheap – but slow

(Trolley) Buses

The city has a comprehensive bus and trolley bus service (1 ruble for any journey; buy tickets from the driver), but because of traffic congestion this is a slow way to travel. Most maps show routes, and bus stops are clearly marked by mustard yellow boards indicating route number and terminus. Take the Metro if at all possible.

Taxis

If you are not going far, finding a cab and negotiating the fare will probably take more time than walking or getting a bus or the Metro. The Moscow taxi business is a kind of free-for-all, with many drivers suspected of being mafia or black-marketeers as well as everything else cabbies are reputed to be. But if you really

want a cab (it could be anything from an official Moscow taxi with a block pattern on the front doors or an ordinary Muscovite looking to earn some extra money), make clear before you drive off where you're going and how much you will be paying. Two words of warning here: don't take gypsy (unlicensed) cab at night, and if you are a woman don' get into a cab with more than one person already in it.

There is a central taxi service and yo can book a cab by calling 927 0000 o 927 2108 at any time of the day or night They will take around an hour to get vehicle to you.

Chauffeur-driven and Limousines

For some time now guys with their ow cars have been offering driving services t foreigners on a daily or weekly (or longer basis. Check the classifieds in *The Moscov Times* for possible candidates. Don't expect luxury, but employing someone (residents here currently pay $50–60 a week will save you a lot of hassle and mak sure you find everywhere you want to go

The more official options are obviousl more expensive, but useful to know about Check out **Intourist** (Tel: 215 6191) fo car rental, with or without driver; **InNis** (a Nissan joint venture), which offers chauffeur service at $16 an hour (Tel 927 1187); and **Autosan** at $13 an hour self-drive (Tel: 280 3600). **Intourservice** has a chauffeured limousine service (Tel: 203 0096); and **Hertz** has an office in town (Tel: 448 8035).

Driving

Unless you're used to cities like Paris, New York or Milan, the simple advice to drivers is don't. Not only is driving on the Moscow road system something like an anachronistic chariot-race but the roads are so bad – pot-holes the size o craters (and those are the good ones) – that you need radar to negotiate them. The GAI (traffic cops) have a well-earned reputation for corruption and there's nothing they like better than flagging down foreigners (car registrations in Moscow tell your life story in a cluster of letters and numbers) and charging them exorbitant fines for real or imaginary offences – they'll charge you less if you don't ask for an official ticket. But if you do bring your own car or rent a foreign make, you'll need to buy petrol vouchers through your embassy for the 95 octane they need (standard for Soviet makes is 76 or 93).

Tourist Information

Intourist is still the place to get information – the main office is in the hotel of the same name on Tverskaya, and most of the major hotels have an Intourist office.

Pick up a copy of *The Moscow Times* as soon as you get into town; it carries theatre and other arts listings as well as a classified section where you can find services such as a driver (plus car) or a guide. There is a plan to produce a quarterly *Moscow Handbook* which would be indispensable for the latest news on restaurants, shops and nightlife.

Tours

Intourist still seems to have the monopoly, and will even take you down into the cellar-archives of the once notorious Lubyanka (KGB headquarters) as well as on run-of-the-mill old chestnuts such as the Kremlin and Metro tours. A few private enterprises have entered the field. Try **Intercar** (Tel: 200 5200), if you fancy a trip down the Moskva in a luxury yacht complete with a bar and Italian snacks. The ship is moored in front of the Ukraina Hotel and departs once a day at 12 noon. An ordinary river-boat trip will cost you a lot less; these leave every 15 minutes from a variety of locations on the river (see *AM Itinerary 3*).

Maps

Good, up-to-date maps of Moscow are hard to come by in Moscow itself. Your best bet is to buy *Falk Moscow City Map*

in advance from a good map shop in your own country. Make sure you buy the most recent edition. Organised tours sometimes supply a map of the area/sight you are visiting.

HOURS & HOLIDAYS

Most offices are open from 9am–6pm, shops stay open later but many close for an hour mid-afternoon. Every shop and café has different 'lunch' times, but opening hours and breaks are always posted on the door. The main post office on Tverskaya opens at 8am and closes at 10pm on weekdays, and 5pm on Saturday, closed Sunday. Museums are generally closed one day a week, and one day a month for cleaning; again these days are posted on the main entrances. All businesses, shops, public services, etc are closed on the following public holidays:

1 January	New Year's Day
7 January	Epiphany
8 March	Women's Day
1 and 2 May	May holiday
9 May	VE Day
12 June	Independence Day
7 November	Revolution Day

ACCOMMODATION

Until the advent of perestroika, by Western standards the hotels on offer were uniformly dirty, with cockroaches or mice, and uncomfortable and expensive. The arrival of a 'market economy' and competition from a number of foreign-run hotels has widened the choices and increased the prices dramatically. There's no such thing as a cheap hotel here – prices range from expensive to very expensive, and your best bet is to book through a travel agency. If you don't want to do that, don't despair. Private enterprise has opened up a new option –

VE Day parade, 9 May

short-let apartments. First the hotels. Price categories are as follows: $ = below US$75, $$ = US$75–150, $$$ = US$150–200, $$$$ = US$200–350, $$$$$ = US$350 and above.

Ex-Soviet Hotels (No joint-venture)

AKADEMICHESKAYA I
Leninsky Prospekt
Tel: 238 0902
Not far from Gorky Park, this is where the Academy of Sciences used to put up their visiting foreign academics. Not much in the way of comfort, but relatively clean and very convenient. Still only open to academics. $

AKADEMICHESKAYA II
Donskaya Ulitsa
Tel: 238 0508
A lot less convenient, much bigger and less attractive all round than its sister establishment. $

LENINGRADSKAYA
Kalanchovskaya Ulitsa 21–40
Tel: 975 3008
Dirt cheap and that's probably what you're paying for – I don't know anyone who has ever stayed here, but the prices are an indication of the room quality. $

MOSKVA
Okhotny Ryad 7
Tel: 292 1100
If you can get in here, you've hit the jackpot. Purpose-built for People's Deputies and visiting VIPs, it's still the preserve of government officials. Beautiful rooms, many overlooking the Kremlin, and excellent (Russian) food. Who says you can't get a decent hotel for a decent price in this city. $

ROSSIYA
Ulitsa Varvarka 6
Tel: 298 5531
Claims to be the biggest hotel in the

Ukraina Hotel

world (more than 5,000 rooms), but that's no recommendation. The Rossiya is an experience in itself. It's more like a small town than a hotel and, though they're trying to go up-market, it's still the same grubby place it always was. However, its location just off Red Square and the views from the upper storeys (there are 21) are a real attraction. $

UKRAINA
Kutuzovsky Prospekt 2/1
Tel: 243 3030
A Stalin wedding cake, this is actually a lovely hotel. It's central, clean, spacious and the rooms are well-proportioned with beautiful wooden floors. $

BELGRAD
Smolenskaya Ploshchad 5
Tel: 248 1643
Comparatively cheap, but that's about all it has going for it. $$

COSMOS
Prospekt Mira 150
Tel: 217 0785
What can you say about the Cosmos? It's big, it's ugly (built by French architects in the early 1970s), it's sleazy, and the bar is a notorious pick-up place. But the rooms are adequate in a Soviet kind of way, and the prices fairly reasonable. $$

The Cosmos, designed by the French

ZOLOTOYE KOLTSO
Smolenskaya Ploshchad 5
Tel: 248 6734
Formerly the Belgrad I, it has had some work done to it. $$

INTOURIST
Ulitsa Tverskaya (formerly Gorky) 3–5
Tel: 203 4008

As the Cosmos, but more central. Only double rooms available. $$$

MEZHDUNARODNAYA I AND II
Krasnopresnenskaya Nab 12
Tel: 253 2382 (I) and 253 2760 (II)
Known affectionately as the Mezh, this hotel and international business centre was built with assistance from financier Armand Hammer in the late 1970s. Though now eclipsed by the Metropol and Savoy, it's still one of the best hotels and the prices reflect that status. $$$$

METROPOL
Teatralny Proyezd 1–4
Tel: 927 6000
If you can afford it, this is *the* place to stay in the city centre. Beautifully renovated by a team of Finns, it is elegant, luxurious and very expensive. Worth every penny. $$$$$

The cavernous Molodyozhnaya

MOLODYOZHNAYA
Dmitrovskoye Shosse 27
Tel: 210 9311
Built out in the sticks as a hotel for groups of visiting school children and pioneers (the Soviet equivalent of boy/girl scouts). Its public areas are cavernous and decorated with the kind of garish mosaics the old regime thought promoted 'brotherhood' among peoples. This place is notorious for its complementary 'house pets', and the food is poor, but price-wise it's not bad. $$$$$

Joint-venture Hotels

NOVOTEL
Sheremetyevo II Airport
Tel: 578 9407
Well, it's a Novotel, and the sound of landing and departing planes add to the

sense that you could be anywhere in the world. $$$

SAVOY
Rozhdestvenka 3
Tel: 929 8500
Formerly the Hotel Berlin, this was the first Western-Soviet joint venture into the hotel business. It's still the preferred place to stay (especially for Scandinavian and Northern European businesspeople), and standards are excellent though the trappings may be rather faded now. $$$

AEROSTAR
Korpus 9, 37 Leningradsky Prospekt
Tel: 155 5030
Canadian/Russian quality hotel, with excellent seafood restaurant. $$$$

MARCO POLO/PRESNAYA
Spiridonyevsky per. 9
Tel: 202 0381
Formerly reserved for Soviet VIPs, it is smoothly run, quiet and luxurious. $$$$

PENTA
Olimpisky Prospekt 18/1
Tel: 971 6101
Outside the city centre, but true to the chain's formula it offers quality to match the prices. $$$$

PULLMAN/IRIS
Korovinskoye Shosse 10
Tel: 488 8080
French chic and very bourgeois comfort. Great restaurants. $$$$

SLAVYANSKAYA/RADISSON
Berezhkovskaya Nab 2
Tel: 941 8020
So new you can still see the paint drying, but it's elegant, well-appointed, and very luxurious. The 24-hour coffee shop in the lobby is a godsend. $$$$

The Radisson

Other Accommodation

Official rental agencies offering flats for short or long lets:

AVANGARD
Ulitsa Byelomorskaya, Fax: 455 9210

RUBIN
Prospekt Mira 24, Tel: 283 1659

YUPITER
Zatzepsky Val 6/kvartira 56, Tel: 235 8675

Chemist's sign

HEALTH & EMERGENCIES

By Western standards (even American), the city's health services are pretty pathetic. There's a doctor on call at all hotels 24 hours a day, but if you are seriously ill, the best thing to do is call a foreign doctor. Before arriving in Moscow, you should make sure you have comprehensive holiday medical insurance which includes evacuation. It may cost a little extra, but it's worth it. Most embassy physicians will only treat staff and their families, so your best bet is to call **The American Medical Center**, Shmitovsky Proyezd 3 (Tel: 256 8212), which is run like a general medical practice in the West. They will provide medical care, pharmacy services, X-rays, tests, and assist with repatriation.

The Medicine Man is a Ciba-Geigy joint venture which will fill perscriptions for hard currency or credit cards; you'll find them on Ul. Pokrovka 4 (Tel: 155 7080). If you're really desperate, you can always go to **Botkin Hospital** at 2-Botkinsky Proyezd 5, Korpus 5 (Tel: 255 0015).

Safety

There was a time when the Soviet authorities claimed there was no crime in Moscow. Glasnost put an end to that myth, but the ensuing openness about crime statistics has generated near-terror in many ordinary Muscovites. The overkill in the media on the realities of big-city life has led some people to feel Moscow now ranks alongside New York in terms of violence and mugging attacks. Although the dangers are increasing, if you use your common sense you shouldn't have any trouble. Take obvious precautions like keeping your valuables in a money-belt and not carrying all your money with you.

Women are advised not to take cabs by themselves, and never to get into a taxi that has more than one person in it. If you're riding the Metro late at night you'll see an official sitting in a kiosk at the bottom of the escalators – wait close by and don't get into a train compartment occupied by only one man or a group of men.

Should you happen to be out alone at night, walk as if you know where you're going, don't keep looking at your map. If you get lost find a militiaman or GAI (traffic cop) and ask directions.

The city's general alarm numbers are:
Fire: 01
Police: 02
Ambulance: 03

COMMUNICATION & MEDIA

The area code for Moscow is 095. Unlike in most other places worldwide, in Russia you don't drop the zero when calling from outside the country. If you want to leave a number with friends/family, then you should give them: 7-095+your number. There are phone boxes located all over the city, and you'll need a 15-kopek piece to make a call. International telephone calls, faxes, telexes, and the other usual postal services are available at the main post office on Ul. Tverskaya 7 (Monday to Saturday 8am–10pm, Sunday 8am–5pm). You cannot make international calls from most phones during the day or evening, but international line

weeklies at kiosks and at the big hotels. *The Moscow Times* was in the process of going daily at the time of writing – look out for it, it will provide you with insights into city politics as well as theatre listings, new restaurants, and so on – it's free. *Moscow Magazine* is a bi-monthly and also includes a pull-out handbook on how to survive the city.

Radio and Television

Gone are the days when mass media were used to bolster authority and the Soviet people's belief in the imminent victory of Communism. The old heavy-duty reports on the decline and fall of the West have now been replaced by *Dallas*, *Eastenders* and other soaps dubbed into Russian. Our news and current affairs programmes reflect the changes this society has undergone in recent years, and are usually objective and authoritative.

The television system broadcasts on four main channels: One and Two are national, Three is the Moscow channel and Four is devoted primarily to educational programmes. You can see the national news on most stations at 9pm nightly.

Radio Moscow has an English-language service alongside its Russian programmes and broadcasts news bulletins on the hour, but most of the city tunes in to one of the FM Western-style stations. Radio Nostalgie Russia (100.5MHz) plays sentimental pop and presents short news clips in both Russian and French; Radio Maximum (103.7MHz) is the channel for Russian pop and rock; it also has gossipy English-language spots on politics and cultural events every 15 minutes. Both are joint ventures and if you want to get into real Russian broadcasting, you'll need a locally produced radio as FM waves can rarely be received on a West-

are opened up for private calls from midnight until 9am, and you can dial direct. The international code is 8-10+country code, area code, number. If you need to call at other times, you can book a call by dialling 8-194 or 196, but you may have to wait in all day for it to come through. There are no US phone credit card facilities in Russia.

For those who don't have the patience, or if there's an emergency, you can pay currency at all the major hotels and at **Alfagraphics**, Ul. Tverskaya 50. They also have fax services, as do the currency **Comstar Business Center** in the Passage Department Store, Ul. Petrovka 10, and ruble **IP Interpret**, who you should call first (Tel: 231 1020).

Newspapers and Magazines

Muscovites have always been avid readers of news. The range today is broader than ever. *Pravda* is still alive and well, the *Moscow News* is less radical than in the early glasnost days; *Izvestya* remains a thorn in authority's side; *Argumenty I Facty* used to be the top investigative paper, but is now rather more sedate; *Ogonyok* was the first paper to understand the implications of Gorbachev's glasnost, and is still authoritative.

If you don't read Russian, you can pick up (often one- or two-day-old) copies of most major Western newspapers and

Reading Russian helps

ern-made set. Evropa Plus (69.8MHz) is the most popular. Of the purely Russian channels ranged between 64MHz and 88MHz, Echo of Moscow is by far the best and Russian speakers will love the talk shows, sound political analysis and intelligent news coverage.

LANGUAGE

Russian is one of the 130 languages used in the former USSR. It is the mother tongue of 150 million Russians and the state language of the Russian Federation.

What usually intimidates people on their first encounter with Russian is the alphabet. In fact it is easy to come to terms with after a little practice, and the effort is worthwhile if you want to make out the names of streets and shop signs.

The Alphabet

printed letter	*sounds, as in*	Russian name of letter
А а	*a*, archaeology	a
Б б	*b*, buddy	be
В в	*v*, vow	v
Г г	*g*, glad	ge
Д д	*d*, dot (the tip of the tongue close to the teeth, not the alveoli)	de
Е е	*e*, get	ye
Ё ё	*yo*, yoke	yo
Ж ж	*zh*, composure	zhe
З з	*z*, zest	ze
И и	*i*, ink	i
Й й	*j*, yes	jot
К к	*k*, kind	ka
Л л	*l*, life (but a bit harder)	el'
М м	*m*, memory	em
Н н	*n*, nut	en
О о	*o*, optimum	o
П п	*p*, party	pe
Р р	*r* (rumbling, as in Italian, the tip of the tongue is vibrating)	er
С с	*s*, sound	es
Т т	*t*, title (the tip of the tongue close to the teeth, not the alveoli)	te
У у	*u*, nook	u
Ф ф	*f*, flower	ef
Х х	*kh*, hawk	ha
Ц ц	*ts* (pronounced conjointly)	tse
Ч ч	*ch*, charter	che
Ш ш	*sh*, shy	sha
Щ щ	*shch* (pronounced shcha conjointly)	
ъ	(the hard sign)	
Ы ы	*y* (pronounced with the same position of the tongue as when pronouncing G, K)	y
ь	(the soft sign)	
Э э	*e*, ensign	e
Ю ю	*yu*, you	yu
Я я	*ya*, yard	ya

Numbers

1	*adín*	один
2	*dva*	два
3	*tri*	три
4	*chityri*	четыре
5	*pyat'*	пять
6	*shes't*	шесть
7	*sem*	семь
8	*vósim*	восемь
9	*d'évit'*	девять
10	*d'ésit'*	десять
11	*adínatsat'*	одиннадцать
12	*dvinátsat'*	двенадцать
13	*trinátsat'*	тринадцать
14	*chityrnatsat'*	четырнадцать
15	*pitnátsat'*	пятнадцать
16	*shysnátsat'*	шестнадцать
17	*simnátsat'*	семнадцать
18	*vasimnátsat'*	восемнадцать
19	*divitnátsat'*	девятнадцать
20	*dvátsat'*	двадцать
30	*trítsat'*	тридцать
40	*sórak*	сорок
50	*pidisyat*	пятьдесят
60	*shyz'disyat*	шестьдесят
70	*s'émdisyat*	семьдесят
80	*vósimdisyat*	восемьдесят

90	divinósta	девяносто
100	sto	сто

Time

What time is it?
katóryj chas? — **Который час?**

hour	chas	час
day	den'	день
week	nid'élya	неделя
month	m'ésits	месяц
Sunday	vaskris'én'je	воскресенье
Monday	panid'él'nik	понедельник
Tuesday	ftórnik	вторник
Wednesday	sridá	среда
Thursday	chitv'érk	четверг
Friday	pyatnitsa	пятница
Saturday	subóta	суббота

Useful Phrases

Hello!
zdrástvuti — **Здравствуйте!**

Good morning
dobrae útra — **Доброе утро**

Good afternoon
dóbry den' — **Добрый день**

Good evening
dobry véchir — **Добрый вечер**

Good night
spakóiniy nóchi — **Ппокойной ночи**

Good bye
dasvidán'ye — **До свидания**

What is your name?
kak vas (tibya) zavút? — **Как вас (тебя) зовут?**

My name is…
minya zavut… — **Меня зовут…**

Do you speak English?
vy gavaríti pa angliski? — **Вы говорите по-английски?**

I don't understand
ya ni panimáyu — **Я не понимаю**

Repeat, please
pavtaríti pazhálsta — **Повторите, пожалуйста**

Thank you (very much)
(bal'shóe) spasíba — **(Большое) спасибо**

Please	pazhálsta	Пожалуйста
Excuse me	izviníti	Извините
Good	kharashó	хорошо

Where is the…?
gd'e (nakhóditsa)…? — **Где находится…?**

bus station
aftóbusnaya stántsyja/aftavakzál — **автобусная станция/автовокзал**

bus stop
astanófka aftóbusa — **остановка автобуса**

airport	airapórt	аэропорт
railway station	vakzál	вокзал
post office	póchta	почта
police station	milítsyja	милиция
embassy	pasól'stva	посольство
consulate	kónsul'stva	консульство
pharmacy	apt'éka	аптека
restaurant	ristarán	ресторан
bar	bar	бар
taxi	taxí	такси
hospital	bal'nítsa	больница
subway station	mitró	метро
supermarket	univirsám	универсам
department store	univirmák	универмаг

Food

mineral water
minirál'naya vadá — **минеральная вода**

juice	sok	сок
coffee	kófe	кофе
tea	chai	чай
beer	píva	пиво
ice	marózhynaya	мороженое
fruit	frúkty	фрукты
salt	sol'	соль
pepper	périts	перец
sugar	sákhar	сахар
beef	gavyadina	говядина
pork	svinína	свинина
chicken	kúritsa	курица
fish	ryba	рыба
shrimp	kriv'étki	креветки
vegetables	óvashchi	овощи
rice	ris	рис
potatoes	kartófil'	картофель
bread	khleb	хлеб
butter	másla	масло
eggs	yajtsa	яйца
soup	sup	суп
sandwich	butyrbrót	бутерброд

The bill, please
shchyot pazhalsta — **Счёт, пожалуйста**

SPORT

Sports Facilities

Football is the summer game and ice-hockey the winter sport in Moscow. The city's major league teams play both at the **Dinamo Stadium** (Leningradskiy Prospekt 36, Metro Dinamo) and at the Luzhniki sports hall (Metro Sportivnaya). Tickets can be bought at the stadia and at booths in Metro stations.

If you can't live without a regular workout, try **Slavyanskaya Radisson**'s health centre and pool, Berezh-Kovskaya Nab 2 (just next door to the Kiyevskaya rail and Metro stations); the Chaika sports centre on Kropotkinskaya Nab. 3/5, which also has a pool and workout equipment (hard currency). The **International Women's Club** organises aerobics, etc, but you'll have to go through your embassy for details.

USEFUL ADDRESSES

Airlines

For Sheremetyevo airport flight information, Tel: 578 7518/7816.

AEROFLOT
Leningradsky Prospekt 37
Tel: 155 7518/156 8019
AIR FRANCE
Korovy Val 7
Tel: 237 2325
ALITALIA
Ul. Pushechnaya 7
Tel: 923 9840
BRITISH AIRWAYS
Krasnopresnenskaya Nab. 12, Floor 19
Tel: 253 2492
CONTINENTAL AIRLINES
Ul. Neglinnaya 15
Tel: 924 9050
DELTA
Krasnopresnenskaya Nab. 12, Floor 11
Tel: 253 2658
IBERIA
Krasnopresnenskaya Nab. 12, Floor 14
Tel: 253 2263
JAPAN AIR LINES
Kuznetsky Most 3
Tel: 921 2846

KLM
Krasnopresnenskaya Nab. 12, Floor 13
Tel: 253 2150
LUFTHANSA
Penta Hotel, Olimpisky Prospekt 18/1
Tel: 975 2501
MALEV
Kamergerskiy Pereulok 6
Tel: 292 0434
SAS
Kuznestsky Most 3
Tel: 925 4747
SWISSAIR
Krasnopresnenskaya Nab. 12, Floor 20
Tel: 253 8988
TWA
Berezhkovskaya Nab. 2, American Business Centre
Tel: 941 8146

Embassies

AUSTRALIA
Kropotkinsky Per. 12, Tel: 246 5012/16
AUSTRIA
Starokonyushenny Per. 1, Tel: 201 7307
BELGIUM
Ul. Malaya Molchanovka 7, Tel: 291 6027
CANADA
Dtarokonyushenny Per. 23, Tel: 241 5070
ESTONIA
Sobinovsky Per. 5, Tel: 290 5013
FRANCE
Ul. Bolshaya Yakimanka 45, Tel: 236 0003
GERMANY
B. Gruzinskaya Ul. 17, Tel: 252 5521
INDIA
Ul. Vorontzovo Pole 6–8, Tel: 297 0820
ITALY
Ul. Vesnina 5, Tel: 241 1533
JAPAN
Kalashny Per. 12, Tel: 291 2707
LATVIA
Chaplygina 3, Tel: 925 2707
LITHUANIA
Pisemskogo 10, Tel: 291 1698

NETHERLANDS
Kalashny Per. 6, Tel: 291 2999
NORWAY
Ul. Prechistenka 7, Tel: 290 3872
SPAIN
Ul. Gertsena 50/8, Tel: 202 2180
SWEDEN
Ul. Mosfilmovskaya 60, Tel: 147 9009
SWITZERLAND
Stopani Per. 2/5, Tel: 925 5322
UNITED KINGDOM
Sofiyskaya Nab. 14, Tel: 231 8511/12
UNITED STATES
Novinskiy Bulvar 19/23, Tel: 252 2451

Tourist Information

Intourist Offices

AUSTRALIA
Intourist Australia Ltd, Underwood House, 6th Floor, 37–49 Pitt Street, Sydney NSW 2000. Tel: 02-247 7652, Fax: 02-251 6196

GERMANY
Intourist Reisen GmbH, Kurfürstendamm 63, 1000 Berlin 15. Tel: 30-88 00 70, Fax: 30-88 00 7126

UNITED KINGDOM
Intourist Travel Ltd, Intourist House, 219 Marsh Wall, London E14 9FJ. Tel: 071-538 8600, Fax: 071-538 5967

UNITED STATES
630 Fifth Avenue, Suite 868, New York, NY 10111. Tel: 212-757 3884/5, Fax: 212-459 0031

FURTHER READING

Non-fiction

Insight City Guide: Moscow, edited by Wilhelm Klein, Apa Publications, 1992. Lavishly photographed guide by Moscow's best journalists and writers.
Discovering Moscow, Helen Boldyreff Semler, Equation, 1989. Not always accurate factually and pretty bulky, but this is considered the best 'companion' guide to the city's architecture.
USSR: from an original idea by Karl Marx, Marc Polonsky & Russel Taylor, Faber & Faber, 1986. Hilarious dissection of Soviet life as it was until very recently.
The New Russians, Hedrick Smith, Random House, 1990. Once proclaimed as the definitive book on modern-day Soviet society, the revised version published after glasnost has dated quickly.
M.W.'s Russia, Martin Walker, Abacus, 1989. Of all the correspondents who have written books on Russia, Martin Walker of *The Guardian* has done the best job. He actually went out into the streets and talked to people long before glasnost.
Living with Glasnost, Andrew Wilson & Nina Bachkatov, Penguin, 1988. A perceptive portrait of young people in Russia written in a period when they were just beginning to speak out.

Fiction

Poems, Anna Akhmatova, Norton, 1983. Considered the century's best poet (even in the West). Her poems strip bare the pomposity of Soviet ideology.
A Part of Speech, Joseph Brodsky, Oxford University Press, 1980. Nobel-prize winning writer who defined the discontent of the Russian people in poetry. Will give you goose-bumps.
The Master and Margarita, Mikhail Bulgakov, Fontana, 1969. Long suppressed in the Soviet Union, it became *the* cult book of the glasnost generation.
On the Golden Porch and other stories, Tatyana Tolstaya, Penguin, 1990. A poignant collection that gives insight into the soul of contemporary Russia.

Blondes in Red Square

Photography	**Jimmy Holmes** *and*
Pages 5B, 18, 22T, 34, 41B,	**Fritz Dressler**
43B, 45T, 48, 51T, 54, 56T, 60B,	
62B, 63, 66B, 69B, 72, 74T, 75B,	
77, 82B, 85B, 89	
12, 13, 15, 16	**Govorukhin**
14	**Gudenko**
23	**Hans Höfer**
6–7	**Robert D Tonsing**
Production Editor	**Erich Meyer**
Language Consultancy	**Anna Benn, Erich Meyer**
Handwriting	**V. Barl**
Cover Design	**Klaus Geisler**
Cartography	**Berndtson & Berndtson**

INSIGHT *pocket* GUIDES

EXISTING & FORTHCOMING TITLES:

Aegean Islands	Ireland	Phuket
Algarve	Istanbul	Prague
Alsace	**J**akarta	Provence
Athens	**K**athmandu	**R**hodes
Bali	*Bikes & Hikes*	Rome
Bali Bird Walks	Kenya	**S**abah
Bangkok	Kuala Lumpur	San Francisco
Barcelona	**L**isbon	Sardinia
Bavaria	Loire Valley	Scotland
Berlin	London	Seville/Grenada
Bhutan	**M**acau	Seychelles
Boston	Madrid	Sikkim
Brittany	Malacca	Singapore
Brussels	Mallorca	South California
Budapest &	Malta	Southeast England
Surroundings	Marbella/	Sri Lanka
Canton	*Costa del Sol*	St Petersburg
Chiang Mai	Miami	Sydney
Costa Blanca	Milan	**T**enerife
Costa Brava	Morocco	Thailand
Cote d'Azur	Moscow	Tibet
Crete	Munich	Turkish Coast
Denmark	**N**epal	Tuscany
Florence	New Delhi	**V**enice
Florida	New York City	Vienna
Gran Canaria	North California	**Y**ogyakarta
Hawaii	**O**slo/Bergen	Yugoslavia's
Hong Kong	**P**aris	*Adriatic Coast*
Ibiza	Penang	

• •

United States: **Houghton Mifflin Company, Boston MA 02108**
Tel: (800) 2253362 Fax: (800) 4589501

Canada: **Thomas Allen & Son, 390 Steelcase Road East**
Markham, Ontario L3R 1G2
Tel: (416) 4759126 Fax: (416) 4756747

Great Britain: **GeoCenter UK, Hampshire RG22 4BJ**
Tel: (256) 817987 Fax: (256) 817988

Worldwide: **Höfer Communications Singapore 2262**
Tel: (65) 8612755 Fax: (65) 8616438

" " I was first drawn to the Insight Guides by the excellent "Nepal" volume. I can think of no book which so effectively captures the essence of a country. Out of these pages leaped the Nepal I know – the captivating charm of a people and their culture. I've since discovered and enjoyed the entire Insight Guide Series. Each volume deals with a country or city in the same sensitive depth, which is nowhere more evident than in the superb photography. **" "**

Sir Edmund Hillary

INSIGHT GUIDES

COLORSET NUMBERS

You'll find the colorset number on the spine of each Insight Guide.

NOTES